The city observed
Notes from an unfolding India

Other titles of interest:

Geographic Information System for Smart Cities

Prof. TM Vinod Kumar and Associates

Metropolitan Governance: Cases of Ahmedabad and Hyderabad

Dr. Vinita Yadav

India's Urban Confusion: Challenges and Strategies

Edited by Dr. M. Ramachandran

Designing Better Architecture Education: Global Realities and Local Reforms

Dr Manjari Chakraborty

The Ekistics of Animal and Human Conflict

Rishi Dev

Water Conservation Techniques in Traditional Human Settlements

Pietro Laureano

Built, Unbuilt and Imagined Sydney

Dr Anuradha Chatterjee

The city observed
Notes from an unfolding India

Pallavi Shrivastava

COPAL PUBLISHING GROUP

Inspiring a better future through publishing

Published by Copal Publishing Group
E-143, Lajpat Nagar, Sahibabad,
Distt. Ghaziabad, UP – 201005, India

www.copalpublishing.com

First Published 2015

ISBN: 978-93-83419-14-2 (hard back)
ISBN: 978-93-83419-18-0 (e-book)

Typeset by Bhumi Graphics, New Delhi
Printed and bound by Bhavish Graphics, Chennai

Contents

Notes and quotes

Mumbai has been city of my belonging. To which I have shared a complex equation.

A city to which I have tried to attach, detach and reattach, but only in most complex ways. The process has been one of difficult learning and unlearning in most profound ways.

Mumbai, as it has been unfolding, rising so to speak both physically and metaphorically. And in doing so, has somewhat undone itself. Now, nothing seems absolute.

No one seems to be sure of anything. All appears impervious. All appears viscous.

***

Quotes:

W.G. Sebald as quoted by Coetzee in Inner Workings

After a walking tour through the region, Sebald or 'I' is hospitalised in a cataleptic state, with symptoms that include a sense of utter alienation linked to hallucination of being in a high place looking down on the world. To this vertigo he gives a metaphysical rather than a merely psychological interpretation, 'If we view ourselves from a great height, it is frightening to realise how little we know about our species, our purpose and our end.

***

V.S. Naipaul in *India: A Million Mutinies Now*

Bombay continued to define itself: Bombay flats on either side of the road now, concrete buildings mildewed at their upper levels by the Bombay weather, excessive sun, excessive rain, excessive heat; grimy at the lower levels, as if from crowds at pavement level, and as if that human grime was working its way up, tide mark by tide mark, to meet the mildew.

***

V.S. Naipaul in *India: A Million Mutinies Now*

We had to walk carefully, picking our way over broken or unmade footpaths. Level or fully made footpaths are not a general Indian need, and the Indian city road is often like a wavering, bumpy, much mended asphalt path between drifts of dust and dirt and the things that get dumped on Indian city roads and then stay there, things like sand, gravel, wet rubbish, dry rubbish: nothing ever looking finished, no kerbstone, no wall, everything in a half-and-half way, half-way to being or ceasing to be.

***

Vincent Scully in *Modern Architecture*

The old, preindustrial, predemocratic way of life has progressively broken away around him so that he has come to stand in a place no human beings have ever quite occupied before. He has become at once a tiny atom in a vast sea of humanity and an individual who recognizes himself as being utterly alone. He has therefore vacillated between a frantic desire to find something comprehensible to belong to and an equally consuming passion to express his own individuality and act on his own.

***

Percy Bysshe Shelley in *Prometheus Unbound*

The wrecks beside of many a city vast,

Whose population, which the earth grew over,

Was mortal, but not human; see, they lie,

Their monstrous works…

***

Salman Rushdie in *Joseph Anton: A Memoir*

When a book leaves its author's desk it changes. Even before anyone has read it, before eyes other than its creator's have looked upon a single phrase, it is irretrievably altered. It has become a book that can be read, that no longer belongs to its maker. It has acquired, in a sense, free will. It will make its journey through the world and there is no longer anything the author can do about it.

***

Jane Jacobs in *The Death and Life of Great American Cities*

No good for cities or for their design, planning, economics or people can come of the emotional assumption that dense city population are, per se, undesirable. In my view, they are assets. The task is to promote the city life of city people, housed, let us hope, in concentrations both dense enough and diverse enough to offer them a decent chance at developing city life.

***

Ada Louis Huxtable in *On Architecture*

Does this mean that the supertall building is doomed? Will the race for the sky stop? Only if human nature changes, and our grand, romantic impulses disappear. We move into the "earthquake proof" buildings that engineers devise after every temblor with the confidence of "lesson learned." We keep the sandbags ready for the next flood. The human capacity to forget and minimize catastrophe, to learn to live with it, ameliorates pain and suffering and anesthetizes memory.

***

Paul Goldberger in *Why Architecture Matters*

But finally architecture is not about itself. It is about everything else. It is never a neutral envelope. It is made to contain something, and to understand architecture fully you have to understand more than architecture.

***

Preface

Any city that has gone through rapid urbanization has had to deal with forces that are unique to the fabric of that very city. Mumbai has been no exception. And to witness the changes that are taking shape in built environment of Mumbai are intriguing, as they reflect the nervous tension of growing anxiety through fractured changes. Through these reflective essays, primarily revolving around architecture and design but, at the same time, not losing perspective of urban design and planning that shape a city, I have put together my observations. Mumbai offers an interesting platform to study and learn for any rapidly growing city which has such cosmopolitan population, richly diverse and yet rooted in culture and history.

The essays presented in this compilation are an attempt to look at Mumbai's built environment with more holistic approach of cultural and social fabric in mind than merely as an architectural feat of ego drive or superlatives of western ideas. Mumbai is no New York. Just like New York is not Mumbai. Hence these comparisons are unfair and we would have to be rather sensitive in aspiring one city to be just like another. Different cities have different underlying currents and forces, unique to only them, and we will have to be mindful of it when we suggest built environment solutions. Similarly, to expect Mumbai to be next Shanghai or Singapore will be a folly, one of homogenisation. Flattening of deep cultural diversity has not excluded architecture and this is becoming increasingly clear with global architectural practices working in India whose design solutions have been vastly similar with respect to use of materials, explorations of forms and aspirations of superlatives of tallest, largest, biggest and so on.

This compilation is an inquiry into some of these issues, which tries to look at architecture, not in isolation, but how it is very much a culturally and socially enmeshed desire and outcome that values diversity and social context. These essays try to bring home a point that architecture is about everything and hence to understand it, it has to be looked at more than just physical outcome. We need to look at slow forces and disruptions that shape it as much as its historical context.

The essays are presented as they were first published on their original platform on a specific day and year without being modified, rewritten and without major edits. In doing so, the idea was to retain the original reflection or point of view at that given timeframe, without passage of time to command a need for them to be restated or revised to emulate more current and changed understanding. Constraints of the platform also reflect the parameters under which these articles were written, as a commentary from a citizen of the city, on architecture and on its 'why' or 'how' with an intention to probe architecture not as an art, a sculpture or a statement, rather an important permanent and semi-permanent space that we inhabit on a daily basis and how it impacts and shapes us even without us being conscious about it.

Foreword

The people of every culture and society involve themselves in a variety of things and professions that lend definition to their lives. For some, it will be the caring for their families or the businesses they have built over years; some sell fruit and vegetables, perform services like pest control, building design, and funerals; while others make sport their profession or steer boats and planes. There are teachers, and there are journalists and newsreaders...and there are writers. Over the years, I have found the act of writing to have been an activity engaged that has consistently affected my life in every way, through which I have discovered the most light-hearted occasions in the pure joy of laughter, to the most profound moments of sadness and depth of feeling for human endeavour.

I am able to read, because there are those who write.

As the most direct and powerful means to understand the soul of another human being, nothing provides more simple or complete access than a book or text. The shallowest being and most callous animal, sensitive, inspiring or incorruptible individual will always be exposed in their writing, provided the words are indeed their own. It is for this reason the people who influence my life most, who have changed me for the better and where it has mattered most, have not been those who make mobile devices and gadgets, cars or food, but those who write. And of writers, the ones who inspire the strongest emotions and convictions also demonstrate the abilities to address issues of truth and the human condition through the strength and integrity of their voices and words – in most respects, critical writing, beyond being simply necessary, is vital conscience and soul of any culture and society, our claim to the right of integrity and truth.

Pallavi shows every promise of being one among a growing number of voices in India that assert this right. Reading through her essays on events, current or continuing, I have sensed a quiet resolve regarding topics both complex and difficult, some of contention, others deserving of it, some yet to find aim; but all fundamentally tied to the specific context of India, the city within which she resides, and the forces of culture and society that shape them both. Be it how bullet holes probe the way to our collective memories, the way violence against women is less a physical act than one of the deepest ignorance, or how one's sense of urban insecurity stems less from the absence of official enforcement than that of societal tolerance of it, Pallavi brings her developing focus less to the problems and issues of contemporary Indian life, than to the sources of them – like the most discerning writers before her, she cares for the elucidation of reasons rather than blame.

It is often said that one does not study or write poetry to be a poet; one does because one already is. In much the same way, Pallavi writes only because she must. My deepest hope is that she will grow with this foundation in her life, and through deepening experience, understanding, and her increasing familiarity with the profound nuance of language, take her writing to join the collective voices that subtly, powerfully, change lives and allow us to take the measure of our humanity, and in ways that only bring more to write.

Kevin Mark Low

Chapter 1

Social fabric and forces for built environment

Women and public spaces in India

Negotiations and its implications in an urban movement

Considered as one of the modern cities in India, Mumbai is a cosmopolitan and home to 5.5 million women. It is celebrated as one of the safest cities for women to live in India. Yet, not a day goes by without a brief in newspaper on woman of any age group or class being molested, attacked, sexually harassed, compromised or violated in some way in the city. With recent debate spurred by the unfortunate incident in Delhi of a 23-year-old girl, being mob-raped in a moving bus then beaten and left to die, it is important to question the forces that lead to this reprehensible behaviour with women and how much of it is facilitated by planned and unplanned urban spaces. Keeping women away from public spaces due to perceived physical threat is common in India. This is very much related to the power equation of different genders articulated through socially coded behaviours, patriarchy and pre-conceived realms of domesticity.

Growing up in Mumbai, I had internalised this as my second nature and what my urban movement was going to be. *"Stay indoors after dark"; "move in herds of friends or male company"; "if group was not feasible at least have company of a known person"; "always be on guard when traveling in public transport or in public"; "question later if the groping, letching, staring, or whistling was accidental or intentional"...* this covert kind of negotiated presence in public spaces is true for most Indian women. Each has devised their own compromised mode of urban movement whether it's going to work, college or just merely going out. The very idea of women out in open urban spaces on their own is not a given where often well-meant protectionism is provided with implicit advice. It is not surprising, then, to not see many women in leadership roles here. In such a deeply ingrained flaw of treating women as secondary citizens, how does India intend to provide equal access to urban spaces outside their homes?

Source: The Global Urbanist, Online. February 2013

Change the behaviour to change the physical environment

Functional infrastructure in the form of safe public transport, toilets, well-lit streets, safe urban spaces remains at the core of the issue. But access to public spaces like promenades, beaches, sidewalks, parks, libraries, and running tracks is required in an inclusive city irrespective of gender, sexual orientation, ethnicity and economic class. An attempt is required to change cultural pattern and legal systems, educating police and local governments to be more responsive to women's concerns and build public trust in these institutions, thus making the city a place of belonging, exploring and seeking pleasure unequivocally. Long-term structural changes in the subversive culture of casting women as secondary by pre-determining their limiting roles of domesticity are required. What we are witnessing in India are isolated and fragmented efforts of secluding the urban issues and creating sanitized 'bubble' development which boast of superficiality. This I call creating city within a city of mixed-used developments like model of traveling in a private car model where you haven't really dealt with the core issues.

Rethinking place-making and redesigning inclusiveness

What does it do to women's role in the society? It compels them to revise, revisit, modify and adjust their plans of being. They negotiate where and when they can go on an everyday basis. They question their clothing choices as appropriate or not and they seek revalidation of their movement. This is a limitation; a limitation of movement and behaviour that has much larger implication of women's role in the society that is already curbed, tailored without realizing their full potential of what they may be capable of achieving. This is strikingly different to what access in public spaces it provides to men. As they grow into adults, they expand and move in urban spaces freely, thus giving them an access to almost any space, any time of the day. This enables men to have more possibilities in moving socially upwards, more freedom in seeking suitable employment and easier access to education. This imbalance with lop-sided access to choices has made women feeling they are less human. We need to radically rethink our goals and then use that as our strength in designing and building spaces that are gender friendly.

React, reclaim, revitalize your urban spaces

That said, it brings us to the question of can we design urban spaces, which are sensitive to everybody? It is probably difficult in only physical sense because it is more cultural, but we have to begin now and make conscious efforts to make it inclusive, just and inviting. Public spaces communicate a city's attitude towards its citizens. Presence of well-designed infrastructure and inviting places are a measure of its extent of inclusiveness. Lack of access not just prohibits the right of women, but also curbs their participation in shaping the future city in which they desire to live; where citizens of all genders can all claim the city with their actual physical self by walking, running, jogging, encountering, strolling, lying on the beach, soaking up the sun and not experience this only through the virtual medium.

I truly believe that India is on the brink of dramatic change. How fostering that change can be is left to the citizens of the country. The time is now.

Leopold Café in Colaba with renewed history

My recent visit to Leopold Café at Colaba Causeway brought back a few uncomfortable memories from the past, of that unfateful day when Mumbai was seized and attacked by terrorists. It was 26th November 2008, which was soon labelled as 26/11 under the burden of sensationalism by earnest media where one's own identity is seen through the western lens even in times of tragedy. American branding had become more essential to the media than the gruesome events that unfolded.

As I sat in the café, sipping my iced tea reminiscing good old college days of being broke and still trying new hangouts. Soon, I was evoked by the memories of the past when Leopold café was attacked leaving 10 people dead right there. It has been 3 years and it made me wonder looking at those bullet marks in the walls, if, with time, we ourselves blur our wounds or wounds themselves dissolve. And how much of it matters of physical traces in built spaces.

The café reopened shortly after the destructive nights of attack. Owners Fahrang & Farzad Jehani defiantly had said, "We would never let terrorists win". The first customer after the reopening, ordered a pint of beer for himself and a Coke for his 6-year-old son, and said Leopold's reopening was a sign "Bombay is getting back to normal".

By maintaining those bullet marks on the walls, the owners have attempted to retain that part of the history and curiosity that many visitors and foreign tourists take a tour and document it through images. In that sense, it may be a continuous reminder of the past.

Leopold café still reeks every bit of its colonial belonging from inside and out. Fluted columns, old cream-coloured slow whirring fans, dark brown partially worn-out furniture, arched windows and semi-wood panelling on the upper walls. Its clientele has always been a mix of foreign tourists, college students and street shoppers. It is always buzzing with activities and is almost never empty and has retained the influx of people to same extent as before the attacks took place.

Source: World Architecture News, online. April 2012

The much talked about fabricated impression of Mumbai's resilience is mostly media generated. People get on and continue with lives often because they may not have luxury of choices. Negative events leave scars on one's mind and carry traces of it for a long time. But what about physical scars such events leave to the built environment? By merely fixing the broken surfaces, painting and giving it a new appearance like nothing ever happened, can we really overcome the past? As Salman Rushdie asks in his book Shame, *"I too face the problem of history; what to retain, what to dump, how to hold on to what memory insists on relinquishing, how to deal with change?"*

Places and people: Journal in transit

If you haven't heard about unfolding of India shining tale yet, you are probably not listening enough. It is probably the single most work of fiction, which many are selling. Not that India is not shining with this newly liberalized state of policies – but it is exclusively so for perhaps 5 percent of its population.

My recent trip to New Delhi just enforced my belief that India is anything but shining for the rest of the 95% of its population, which lives right under a shadow cast by this light.

I got out of the new Indira Gandhi International Airport (designed by Woodhead) and was received by a pre-scheduled driver for me – a young boy who didn't look more than 18/19 years of age, slender and undernourished. Walking along towards the car, he reached out for my bag without looking up. I declined saying *"it's not heavy, don't worry"*. His subservient demeanour was something he has perhaps accepted and internalized as part of what comes with living on the fringes. He didn't speak much and only answered in monosyllables to my queries on distance and travel time while navigating through Delhi roads.

Next, I embarked on to a glitzy Taj Palace at Sardar Patel Marg. The hotel is old and looks a little worn-out now but still carries the grandeur that Taj has made their reputation in luxury section world-wide. Later, inside the restroom, after washing my hands I was accosted by a short, thin young girl staff of Taj, with a ceramic tray carrying a neatly folded napkin with a purple flower on the side. But it occurred to me, while taking the napkin, that I might as well had just picked it up from the stack myself... did I really need her assistance? A question that surfaced for her was whether this is something she really enjoyed doing..., offering guests hand towels on a tray with a flower and slipping in a 'thank you' and remain inside that enclosed space of a restroom during all her working hours? May be that luxury of preferences hadn't crossed her mind.

While heading back to Mumbai, I was a bit rushed and nervous to miss my flight that all thoughts and observations had vanished.

Source: World Architecture News, online. November 2012

But entering Mumbai, I had one last enduring meet of the day with my cab driver, who, to my surprise, was a woman – unusual for Indian soil. Being tired, I kept quiet and just wanted to observe her mannerisms driving the cab on Mumbai's ruthless traffic and road conditions. But it was not to be.

She was a mother of two young kids and looked quite young with a voice that carried traces of frustration. She takes care of a family of four. Her husband died abruptly about 4 years ago in a road accident. Until then she was a housewife but that event triggered her to look for work, which would give her income to survive. She went on to lament that she makes about 300 to 400 INR on a decent day and about 600 to 700 INR on rare better days. But there are days, like Mumbai bandhs (strikes) and festivals when people don't go out much resulting in drying up her daily wages completely. And those days get difficult to manage. Being a woman driver has its own perils, she mentioned. But then she went on to say that she is sending both her kids to school that will ensure better days in future. Amen to that.

These are perhaps India Shining's stepchildren who can see the light from a distance but not glow in it. These are India's misfits who haven't been able to transition successfully into wealth camps of rapid urban development. They have either failed or at best remain displaced far away from opportunities that could have trickled down to them as well with an inclusive system.

A homeless woman in the maximum city

Homelessness is described as a state where certain population of a city is without a legal dwelling. Such people, often unable to acquire and maintain regular, safe and adequate housing, or lack fixed, regular, and adequate residence may inhabit either a government or non-government provision. Each country has its own definition and provisions for homeless people, and solutions to accommodate them varies as well.

Mumbai is a home to countless homeless people and the number stretches in staggering millions. And to see people living on roadside, railway tracks in squatter settlements or a temporary makeshift arrangement are so common that it subverts the convoluted concept of world-class city. The ratio of citizens living in a legal dwelling to illegal one is skewed and the city has lived with it for so long that it has become a part of the city's identity. Something akin to living with shame, live with it for long and it may turn perennial from temporal.

I see one such homeless woman almost every day on my walk to the gym. She appears to be a young woman, with attractive demeanor, deep black eyes and dark sunburnt glowing skin. She mostly wears shorts, short skirts and western attire – quite a departure for what one expects from a homeless Indian woman, living on the streets. I have often seen her solving crossword puzzles or reading a newspaper sitting on that degraded sidewalk. But whatever the activity she is involved in, she is never distressed or looks depressed. On the contrary, she looks comfortable and at peace.

After noticing her for few months, I started to understand her presence. My initial reaction to it was that she is a woman and all by herself on the streets of Mumbai and it must be scary. I had argued to myself, this must be fine in daytime because streets are mostly crowded. My arrogant pity that usually comes with privileged understanding thought of deserted night time when she must be all

Source: World Architecture News, online. May 2012

by herself. She doesn't look perturbed as I would have expected her to be, maybe she isn't. Either way, the trouble I felt towards her was my own, generated in my head. I looked at her from my perspective and subconsciously judged her helplessness, because she is after all, homeless. May be she is not helpless at all. May be, I am the helpless one on the different side of the equation trying to judge her presence and find a solution earnestly.

And that brought me to a basic question: Where is woman really safe? In her house, alone, with people, behind locks, in groups, during daytime, nighttime or in public spaces? Or is there really a place and time where she cannot ever be violated or victimized?

Her calm defies all my mundane worries of her safety and survival. To me, she looks like she landed homeless and has made peace with it in her own way. She appears in absolutely no need to be organized in a civil society of legalized housing and be an actor in this modern world just like others, which is equally wretched, if not more. The world that is roughly and brazenly defined by laws, systems, societies and its moral code of conduct never misses a chance to fail humanity. Who decides that the other side is misplaced with displaced ideas of organizing ourselves in a system?

In that vein, it is important to think beyond our pre-conceived notions of women's safety regardless of her being a homeless person.

Chapter 2

Mumbai's built environment books and beyond

Book review: Why Loiter? Women & Risk on Mumbai Streets

The book *Why Loiter? Women & Risk on Mumbai Streets* aims to map the exclusions and negotiations that women of various age groups and economic classes encounter in their everyday lives in urban spaces of Mumbai. Author trio, Shilpa Phadke, Sameera Khan and Shilpa Ranade have based this book on 3 years of qualitative research and conclude that women's presence and participation in public spaces and events has certainly increased but the city still does not offer them an equal claim into the realm of public safety in urban streets and spaces.

The book embarks on a significant journey on how a radically transforming city (with respect to infrastructure and rapid construction), still continues to grant women a status of only a secondary citizen, by denying them complete safety at any time of the day. Provision of safety in urban spaces encompasses different understanding for women belonging to different economic classes. A woman travelling in a private vehicle from destination A to B has different safety levels offered than another woman travelling from same destination A to B using public transport.

As presented in the book, low visibility areas, poorly lit spaces, deserted streets and public transportation after sunset – all consitute for unsafe environments. To counter this, women alter their movement and restrict accessing urban spaces, maintaining a compromise. The book further presents scenarios where this aspect of women in public spaces is so deeply entrenched that it becomes their second nature to modify their behavior. Examples like covering their chest with a book, file or dupatta, walking while gazing down and pretending to be on the phone while moving swiftly away into private spaces are common glimpses.

What is curious about the book is that it investigates various economic and communal settings and how each is unique in providing different degree of freedom and social constraints. So a city, essentially an amalgam of various faiths and religions/cosmoplitan in

Source: World Architecture News, online. January 2012

its claim, provides different levels of freedom in varied communities. And women are not free from clutches of moral policing, in the name of safety. She can be letched, eve-teased, groped, stared and made to feel voilated, possibly anywhere. On the other hand, same does not apply for men, as the authors point out. Men, move about and expand their access to urban spaces more vigorously and more importantly any time of the day. Thus enabling more choices with respect to jobs they take up or engage in various social gestures.

The book presents scenarios of Mumbai's changing landscape and how this emerging urban fabric could be flawed from equitable development and equal access to all citizens. And this is where I see the authors blurring issues of gender humiliation to urban development. These two are distinct issues and a organic development, devoid of zoning, may not be a solution, as suggested by the researchers. Women's safety in a city is not an unique Indian issue. Its rampant presence here could be a case of cultural baggage of gender hierarchy and its related perils.

Book review: Behind the Beautiful Forevers

I long resisted reading this book. I knew this book chronicles the much too real squalor and marginalized population that Mumbai lives with, and with alarming peace and regularity. On one hand, there is this seemingly globalized progressive glossy world of *Lakme Fashion Weeks* and on the other is the world of cheap labour that performs countless menial works to keep the richer rich by moving and inhabiting themselves in squalid conditions. I have had my ruthless share of V.S. Naipaul's trilogy on India as well.

But after multiple references, I gave up and made my way to Boo's pages.

Boo has restricted her book entirely to a suburban slum that adjoins ever-expanding Mumbai International Airport, Annawadi. Annawadi that started settling since 1990, now faces a threat from an enterprising "shining India" that needs luxury hotels and a world-class airport. But does ambitious development mean displacement of residents of Annawadi? For where will they really go, when their land is taken by an expanding airport and its luxurious expectations? Katherine Boo focuses her ethnographic study on this single urban slum, which she calls the "undercity" – an undercity that is discretely placed as a bitter side dish under the complicated layers of urbanization. And hence, as she puts the issue in her words, "In every community, the details differ, and matter". Certainly. So yes, her book is a detailed one, tirelessly descriptive but not pioneering one, so to speak. But Boo is not claiming it to be that, only media is.

The book portrays closely observed inhabitants of Annawadi, which range from garbage-pickers, garbage-sorters, and garbage-stealers – primarily scavengers of the city. With that, Boo weaves an intricate story of envy-driven Fatima Shaikh who somehow manages a vengeance plot against a young boy named Abdul, a rag picker, who she has accused of a gruesome crime. It does not end with anything definitive, except the complex multi-layered, rich and detailed portrayal.

Source: World Architecture News, online. May 2012

This is perhaps the most striking feature, where Boo never gets pedantic offering sympathy and pity and most importantly any patronizing solutions. Her strength lies in honest, penetrative yet invisible eyes, which are grasping every detail of events and texture of Annawadi. It presents the larger issue of organic urban settlements and their exclusion perils for those who missed the development train. One may call it heartless and cruel, but Boo doesn't do that. She is busy describing endlessly the layers of this complex settlement, which is a microcosm of change, through urbanization that is looming large on Mumbai.

There are difficult issues with extremely uncomfortable questions to be raised. Perhaps it's not about poverty-struck survival martyrs anymore but a collective failure of policies that were ineffective or, more importantly, non-existent.

Katherine's painstaking portrayal of lives of Annawadians shatters the myths of a progressing financial capital of India and it hints (non-glamorously) at what lays in its broken system. The corrupt system, which somehow fails only the poor and their poverty, and whose lives are an embarrassment to this modernizing city of Mumbai. Will they be left behind and crushed to anonymity or confined and hidden away behind the walls like the trash they collect and sort for this other, glitzy India?

Marginalia: Of books and its spaces

Jorge Luis Borges once said, "I have always imagined that paradise will be some kind of library". Library or a thoughtful bookstore can be almost a space – just like paradise. I have never been to paradise myself but, in my imagination, this is what I perceive it to be... a place, where I can spend substantial time browsing, reading passages, making notes, occasionally inhaling the intoxicating smell of paper in those books.

If one has gone around walking in Fort area of Mumbai, near Church gate and Flora Fountain in the past, this area used to be dotted with multiple street book vendors. They stocked old and new (pirated) copies of books. You would stumble on large stacks of Sidney Sheldon and Mills & Boons. But if you looked more closely and browsed more patiently, there was a chance you will be holding an old copy of a good book too. During recent times, these book vendors were cleared by Brihanmumbai Municipal Corporation (BMC), in an effort to clean sidewalk encroachment. It feels like some intrinsic characteristic of old Bombay has been stripped away and failed to compensate with anything equal or better at the same time.

Recently, Mumbai is seeing a rise (and fall too) in chain of commercial bookstores to more honestly curated bookstores. Kitabkhana is one such effort and has been quite popular amongst book lovers. Kitabkhana, housed in one of the heritage buildings of Fort area on M.G. Road, maintains the charm and laid-back characteristics of old times.

The bookstore maintains all the heritage building features such as wrought iron balusters, handrails and decorative columns. Dark wood panelling matches the wood colour of bookshelves which look non-fussy and functional. The kids section of the book has brightly coloured bean bags and that is where experimentation with colours ends. Thankfully, it works well for the purpose. The bookstore also houses a mezzanine level and is more generous with seating at this level.

Source: World Architecture News, online. June 2012

Commercial bookstores usually do not provide lavish and comfortable seating arrangements to avoid books browsers to camp in their facility. For reading pleasure for long hours, you are expected to head to a comfortable and functional library. Unfortunately, Mumbai lacks a good public library facility. Just like lack of any other public space, libraries are not even a consideration in this commercially booming real estate market of Mumbai.

If one has to believe Salman Rushdie's words in how lives are made, then Mumbai's book facilities need to bolster with more rigour and determination and look beyond office buildings and high-end residential construction. And to quote Rushdie's words, "This is how lives are made. But not only in this way, also by dog-eared books discovered accidently at home".

Chapter 3

Urban planning/ design and outcome in infrastructure

Tryst with Mumbai's urban planning

Few days ago, I was headed to Nirlon Knowledge Park in Goregaon, located adjacent to Western Express Highway in Mumbai. It is usual for me to be accompanied by anxiety when I am on the roads of Mumbai. There is certain amount of apprehension that it comes with and reasons are several: unregulated traffic, potholes, no lane system, no explicitly marked exits and entries, and lastly, ambiguous signages.

Having said that, I was joyous to not hit any traffic jams, yet. I had covered my usual ride of 40 minutes in 20 minutes. Just as I was about to get optimistic of Mumbai road travel, I had to step back and reconsider my judgement. To begin, there is no clear indication on where to exit the highway, so as luck would have it, I had missed the exit to Nirlon Knowledge Park. I was worried but the driver said not to worry. He slowed down and looked right and gingerly moved on to service road by going over the broken curb. So with few bumps, I was headed towards my destination.

Entering the campus was easy. I had to go to building number B-2 and there were no signage to point me in the right direction. So, I took the usual mode of human intervention and asked the security guards. They just lift their arm perpendicular to their legs and guide you left and right, whichever direction you should be headed towards. I had to turn left.

Just as I had moved 3 or 4 m, I was stopped by different set of security guards. He made some irrelevant queries and handed me a receipt to get a signature from the person I was going to meet. As I moved ahead, I could see clearly marked building B-3 and logic suggested me B-2 next to it. But in Mumbai you should just keep your logic aside. So, I sought human intervention yet again and a guard pointed to that building.

Once you are inside any Mumbai building, you soon realize, each is guarded like a fortress. The security clearance formalities make you feel less human. I handed my card, the lanky guy behind the desk sent a security code to my cell phone, which I had to produce back.

Source: World Architecture News, online. July 2012

One step cleared. Next, he took my picture. Another one. Lastly, he issued a visitor's pass, which would allow me to enter the lobby, which was again guarded by security personnel. I finally made it to the office where a guard made me enter my details in his roster. Sigh.

While returning, I missed giving the signed receipt to the security guard but I got out of the campus all right. Once, I was out on the road again, it made me ponder about the abundant disagreeable redundancy of security enforcements. I wondered about ceaseless amount of human intervention for way finding and signages and its inefficiencies.

I still have that duly signed receipt in my bag and if it meant anything sincere, I must have breached the security of Nirlon Knowledge Park, Goregaon, Mumbai.

Walking project

Walking is perhaps the most basic activity for human beings. Connectivity of a community within comfortable walking distance to basic amenities is not only sustainable, but also a practice towards healthy well-being. World over, cities are trying to reinvent their urban spaces to reclaim this practice by encouraging better pedestrian connectivity and encouraging walking or bicycle usage to reach places. Unfortunately, in Mumbai, the neighbourhood development has never accounted for wide pedestrian walkways and whatever little is provided is mostly littered, trashed and abused to an extent where citizens would rather hop into a car and go places than risk putting their feet in muck and garbage by pushing and jostling in chaotic spaces.

Walking Project

Walking Project, an initiative by Rishi Aggarwal, Amar Deshpande, Pramod Dabrase, Abhijit Mehta and Vivek Gilani aims to reclaim this

Source: World Architecture News, online. September 2012

basic amenity by making walking a pleasant and environment-friendly feature. Through this initiative, they would like to make Mumbai city the most walkable city in next 10 years.

The project, which is going to be launched during United Nations Conference on Sustainable Development, is an encouraging one for a city where walking comes with its own set of perils. Safety, cleanliness, maintenance, clear demarcation, encroachments are all extremely real issues at play.

Walking Project

Such an initiative, to be successful and widely acceptable, will have to move beyond activism levels and inclusion of well-laid policies and implementation along with sound urban planning. Not to mention, discouraging single occupancy vehicles, strengthening public transport system and decongesting first and then regulating urban pockets will encourage people to walk to places. Unless it is implemented as a holistic strategy where everyone feels they have a role in improving a civic life and reclaiming public spaces, it will remain a challenging task to accomplish.

It is, nevertheless, a significant move towards saner practices leading to a vibrant neighborhood. It is tragic that citizens have to take this matter in their own hands because city officials, bureaucrats, builders and built environment professionals see Mumbai only as a goldmine for making quick money by making it a single-dimensional profit-making commercial or high-density residential tower development.

Brihanmumbai Municipal Corporation promotes cluster redevelopment

Mumbai's civic governing body, Brihanmumbai Municipal Corporation (BMC), has been promoting cluster redevelopment plans for dilapidated buildings, which constitute as many as 70 percent of all buildings in Mumbai. These buildings were built around 35–40 years ago (or more) and most of them as individual projects. While there is still an overarching vision missing for the *Maximum City*, unsafe and worn-out old buildings have been going through piecemeal redevelopment. This gives builders an opportunity to add more floors, as permissible by BMC and hence making it a lucrative endeavour. But this approach has completely missed integrated development.

To counter this, BMC has been promoting cluster development which effectively will take cluster of buildings or neighbourhood and develop it in such a way that it is inclusive of sidewalks, play areas, shops, and other amenities as required. Officials at BMC point out that "The cluster redevelopment policy is aimed at urban renewal and not just redevelopment of old and dilapidated buildings, which is inclusive of upgrading existing infrastructure and adding new ones as necessary". The BMC commissioner has also set up a sub-committee to draft guidelines to incorporate comprehensive development plan for clusters. The sub-committee has had two meetings to further flush out the details of the policy and intends to rollout a pilot project as case study. The results of such a pilot project will enable the officials to come up with recommendations and policy guidelines.

There is a subdued acknowledgement that isolated redevelopment projects are missing something fundamental like a planning vision. In Mumbai it is strangely unique that infrastructure addition and development, mixed or otherwise, are taking shape at the same time, although with fragmented effort. Social forces are more turbulent, rapidly changing and if there is a long-term vision like well-thought cluster planning supplemented with robust infrastructure and basic amenities, there would be better chances of dealing with urbanization in a holistic way.

Source: World Architecture News, online. March 2012

Proposed Bhendi Bazaar Cluster Redevelopment [*Courtesy:* Saifee Burhani Upliftment Trust]

Cluster development would happen in phases but with a blueprint in place and guidelines concretized, individual developer manoeuvring them will be minimized. Clusters can be expanded to more than one and will force developers to abide by the requirements of amenities and spaces as stipulated. Cluster developments provide benefits of better open spaces, internal roads, and connectivity to basic amenities like schools, primary care hospitals and grocery stores. This would prove cost-effective to developers while providing better living standards to tenants and would be much simpler for BMC to monitor project progress.

There is a procedural caveat in this: project affected persons (PAPs) secure alternate living arrangement only in redevelopment of dilapidated buildings. Such provision is not available to PAPs of *cluster development* from governing body. And BMC can play a key role to provide concessions to PAPs and developers who comply to *integrated development* or else they will shy away from something more sensible with higher chances of success for Mumbai.

Nouveau riche and single-occupancy vehicles

I recently heard about one of my acquaintances buying a new sports version of BMW, the Z4. There were celebrations in order! He has progressed to this fancy car as an up-gradation from Mercedes Benz. Recently, there have reports floating about how India's rich are relatively untouched by global economic downturn and the above-mentioned case seems to be from that niche class.

It's a beautiful car and anyone would be happy to own one. More so an Indian, where material possessions like house and car go deep with their identity, of their being. It's a critical aspect and a focal point which elevates one's social status considerably. Hence, I was not surprised that he invited his entire set of friends for a get-together to announce his latest swanky possession. After all, it's a unique status symbol, particularly in the Indian context. Another interesting aspect that I have observed with Indians is that they always overstate the actual value of the possession. They inflate the actual price and mark it up considerably. So a car which was actually of INR 65 lakhs is told to be 95 lakhs. It's a benign habit but deeply entrenched and it reflects deep-rooted insecurities and how important it becomes to do so to gain recognition through materialistic progress amongst their peers and social setting.

With all that said, the point I really wanted to bring out was how misplaced a concept of driving a fancy car is in Indian urban context. Dismal condition of roads, congestion, crowd, traffic, irregular safety norms…all amount to absolutely no driving pleasure, no matter how fancy the car may be. In number of cases, I have seen rich people keeping their fancy cars neatly parked in their garages because it is challenging to get it out on the roads.

Perhaps, India is not meant for single-occupancy vehicles. And it probably never will be, with the current and projected population growth. You can either have enormous population or single occupancy vehicle lifestyle, but not both. It is physically impossible and practically not feasible.

Source: World Architecture News, online. July 2012

India stands at an inflection point with screaming needs to define our urban aspirations. We need to radically think of ways out of single occupancy vehicle concept in comparison to public transport. Incapable of solving larger public transport issues, incompetent governing bodies have left this issue to take its own shape in its own organic way.

Moving forward, it is only going to get worse. Decongesting urban spaces will become even more critical and influx of variety of cars will just not pass as an aspirational concept.

It's interesting to note that all cars, whether manufactured, imported or otherwise, in their advertisements never present the real road conditions of Indian cities. They shoot their ads either in the outskirts of the city or even in another country altogether. It's sad to note the actual conditions are being fudged. But Indians seem to be under a spell of confused euphoria where they are willing to overlook reality just to own a piece of imported concept of car ownership and indianizing that by hiring drivers to drive it for a measly salary.

We are a nation embodied by abundance of cheap labour with expensive habits.

Mumbai urban design competition for Kalanagar traffic junction winners announced

Mumbai Environmental Social Network (MESN), in collaboration with Solomon Guggenheim Foundation, had launched a design competition in November 2012 seeking redesign of Mumbai's busiest and most congested traffic junction, Kala Nagar, near Bandra–Kurla Complex. The competition, administered by Lord Cultural Resources Private Limited, overlooked by Trupti Amritwar Vaitla of BMW Lab, and supported by Vivek Phansalkar, Joint Commissioner of Police (Traffic) of Mumbai, was open to students and professionals. It challenged applicants to restructure the junction's traffic flow and explore ways to reimagine its infrastructure with new public spaces, pedestrian flow and function. A jury that included former Bogotá mayor Enrique Peñalosa and Mumbai traffic police commissioner Vivek Phansalkar selected the top five projects from a pool of 43 total entries from professionals and students from urban design profession worldwide.

The selection committee awarded three honors in the professional category and two in the student category. A "people's choice" winner, selected from either category, was decided by more than 200 community votes at the skywalk of the Kala Nagar Junction and visitors to the Lab at the Dr. Bhau Daji Lad Museum.

About the winning entries:

In the professional category, winner Radhika Mathur presented a plan featuring a pedestrian skywalk and dedicated bus lanes; Sweta Parab and Hrishikesh More designed a series of circular pedestrian promenades; and Mayuri Sisodia and Kalpit Ashar proposed weaving together multiple modes of transportation on two floating, angular islands.

Source: World Architecture News, online. January 2013

Proposed redesign by Radhika Mathur

In the student category, Andres Perez and his group suggested a wide, tree-shaded pedestrian plaza; while a team from the D.Y. Patil College of Architecture included an elevated pedestrian walk with seating and concessions tucked under the flyover.

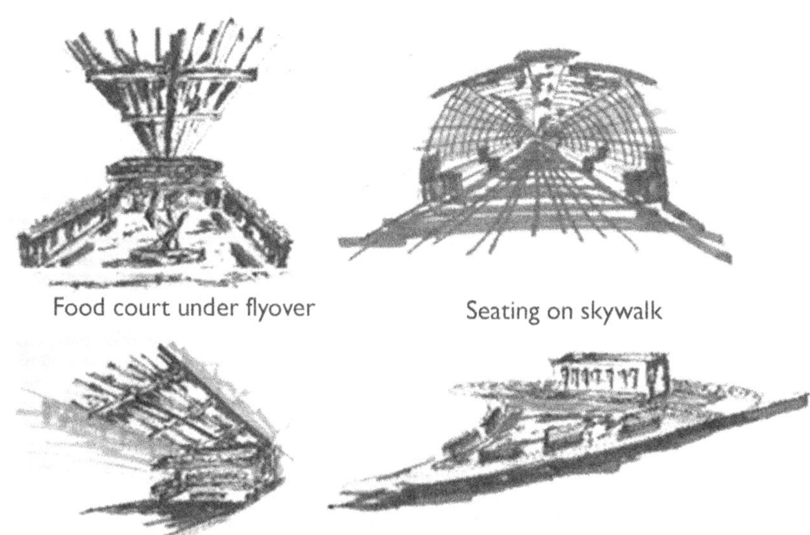

Food court under flyover

Seating on skywalk

Newspaper kiosk under flyover

Designed landscape at bird's feed

Proposed redesign by students of D. Y. Patil College of Architecture, Mumbai

And lastly, the competition also presented a people's choice award to Vedika Tulsiyan, Jaynish Shah, and Karan Sancheti, who proposed an ambitious pedestrian ramp with bleacher seating capped by an elevated, gable-roofed garden.

Now the question to Mumbai is: Which entry should be selected and implemented to actually solve the problem? Is it going to be one picked by the citizens or the one chosen by esteemed panel of judges?

CRIT Mumbai participates in Audi Urban Future Initiative

Collective Research Initiatives Trust (CRIT) is a group of individuals that delves into understanding of urban realm of Indian cities through research and pedagogy. The group was conceived in 2003 and since then, through its activities, has studied and participated in initiatives like housing, urban mapping and various issues in emerging urbanization. The group recently participated in the Audi Urban Future Initiative Awards of 2012 where it stood as one of the four finalists. The competition was won by Boston-based practice, Höweler + Yoon Architecture. The winning entry was a re-imagination of the Interstate I-95 corridor between Boston and Washington D.C. into a mega-region called 'Boswash'.

When CRIT was invited to participate in the Audi Urban Future Award 2012, they were posed these questions: What will the future of Mumbai look like in 2030? What will CRIT's role will be in this envisaged future? And what is its vision?

Below is the CRIT's response for the award, as quoted from Audi Urban Future Initiative website:

On urban futures. Ideas about future cities have been dominated by two imaginations: First, of a utopian coherence unified by robust information systems and coordinated by super infrastructure; and second, a city engendered by catastrophes of environment, poverty, and deterioration. Inherent in these imaginations of coherence and catastrophes is the idea of time as a singular linear rhythm, of space as an entity with fixed coordinates and of people as homogeneous and inert mass. The city, on the contrary, multiplies time(s), blurs boundaries, mixes categories, provides platforms, builds connections, and opens up probabilities to transact–creating possibilities for divergent future trajectories. To talk of "a" future for cities, be it utopian or dystopian, forecloses the possibilities that cities open.

On urban mobility. When mobility is seen as transport, it ends up in a problem-solving exercise that produces either mega

Source: World Architecture News, online. January 2013

projects, intelligent vehicles, or infrastructures that claim to be intelligent. Within the urban realm, the concept of mobility needs to be understood beyond transportation, as transportation itself is embedded in the multiple processes that shape the city. For CRIT, mobility is a twofold concept. First, it involves the different kinds of movements that are brought about by urban transformations today. These include access, migration, gentrification, class movement, etc. And second, mobility or to mobilize is the ability to navigate the complex urban ecosystem of geographies, legislations, claims, powers, relationships, and information to construct one›s path amidst these movements.

This response is a little open-ended and perhaps can be dealt in the second generation of problem solving. While it points out few classic issues clearly but it doesn't point to clear step-wise way forward. At this point, Mumbai does have few glaring issues that can be dealt with a sense of emergency. In my observation, I have seen number of emerging think tanks studying Indian urban issues which are largely multi-layered and complex. They are not being broken down to smaller manageable tangible projects, which could solve some immediate issues facing the cities. Discourse and research can continue, but there is a need to spell out actions and act on them right away through small and medium enterprises, largely enabled through governance.

One, I can say, is mobility and transport: curbing private and single-occupancy vehicles supplemented with robust mass-transit system. Secondly, walking and biking friendly roads and lanes are imperative; clusters of mass functional housing near business corridors is another; and lastly, cleaner and safer Mumbai will require waste management strategy, more public and open spaces, public amenities like libraries, parks and so on. The current fragmented approach of exclusivity and divisive approach will only lead to conditions for corruption and crime. Intervention is necessary and organic and romantic ideas are not an answer to Mumbai's visible plague. The time is now.

Chapter 4

Open and public spaces in dense urban sprawls

Bandra–Worli Sea Link promenade gets a facelift

Mumbai, starved of open and public spaces, both planned and unplanned, will always welcome development of any sort of public space. So the news of Bandra–Worli Sea Link Promenade, an urban development upgrade of a promenade is refreshing. The promenade promises to give a complete makeover to a piece of land lining the sea side from Mahim causeway to the Bandra–Worli Sea Link.

Public Spaces I

While providing a highly upgraded iconic promenade, it promises to house a jogging track, seating and a couple of amphitheatres. It aims at catering to all age-groups at various times of the day. So, people can use it for running, morning walks, informal theatre and even gathering together for a cause. Such spaces serve as essential relief spots in a very congested and dense urban sprawl, and my guess is people would throng to a space like this.

Source: World Architecture News, online. February 2012

The promenade stretches approximately 1.5 km long and runs about 40 m in width. The upgrade process of the promenade is an answer to the growing need to have more functional public spaces where people can breathe fresh air in a congested city like Mumbai. The project cost is estimated at INR 9 crores and local Architect, Nikhil Gore, has designed this urban addition. He proudly ascertains that the project will house Dubai-style glass structures and canopies spread all over the promenade for shading and relief to make a statement. The work at the site has been stalled once already and has picked up again after substantial procedural delay. It's slated for completion in March of the year 2014.

Public Spaces 2

Mumbai is a coastal and a linear city. And having hot and humid weather most of the year, seaside hangouts have been naturally popular amongst its inhabitants. In my experience, due to lack of maintenance and cleanliness, beachfronts in Mumbai have always received a mixed response. Keeping it accessible to all citizens equally and maintaining its cleanliness regardless to economic classes has always been a conflict. How this new Bandra Promenade will fare on this front is yet to be seen. In any case, it remains a noteworthy urban space addition proposal to neutralize the one-dimensional boom in commercial and residential development. To stimulate holistic growth of a city, it is essential that it is one that promotes multi-layered and mixed use developments where public and private spaces are more uniformly available to its inhabitants. Hopefully, such a development will trigger more productive debate leading to additions of thoughtful urban public spaces well integrated in the blue print of Mumbai alongside skyscrapers, malls and lavish hotels.

What Mumbai has in store as a city for its citizen beyond the commercial architecture, once development has reached a substantial stage, remains to be seen. Nevertheless, it provides the city officials an opportunity where thinking holistically about the infrastructure and development, which currently is sorely missing, can make Mumbai a truly healthy city.

Public Spaces 3

Marine Lines promenade phase-II facelift

If one has driven past the Queen's Necklace at Marine Lines, they are likely to momentarily forget all the treachery and dichotomy that the Maximum City holds in its belly. One side of Marine Lines promenade is dotted with Nariman Point's skyline while on the other side is the calm sea, a quiet witness to all the turmoil and promises the city holds. One can behold the dusk view of Queen's Necklace, giving a sense of transient belonging to the city they share a complicated relationship with.

The state government had taken up the initiative to revamp this approximately 3 km stretch of land creating paved footpath, new bus shelters and addition of green beds. This does help. It has given the stretch a lot more clean and accessible areas for the citizens. That was Phase I, where the area covered was from National Centre for the Performing Arts (NCPA) to Girgaum Chowpatty, and the cost incurred was INR 27 crores.

However, Phase II of the revamp is a bit more ambitious and has been embroiled in a series of discussions between architects, local residents committees/ NGOs and Mumbai Metropolitan Region Development Authority (MMRDA), over what the eventual public space should achieve. There is a proposal to include promontory, making its way into the sea with a stepped amphitheatre, a grand forecourt foreclosing government buildings like Mantralaya and Vidhan Bhavan, an open air amphitheatre at Chowpatty, an eco-walk, toilets and drinking water facilities. The cost estimated for this revamp is tagged at INR 100 crores.

Now, while I understand the involvement of citizens in claiming how their public spaces should look and function, I still hold my reservation on how it will actually accommodate many viewpoints of a diverse population. This is a public space and if only the viewpoint of residents in the vicinity is considered, it might end up overlooking needs of several other people who come here from far off locations

Source: World Architecture News, online. March 2012

such as college students, office employees and tourists. Taking only the residents into account becomes exclusive. Although, taking everyone's opinion is simply not possible for the sheer nature of diversity of opinions and ideas that it will generate. The government is ill-equipped to draft a futuristic, inclusive blueprint of this public space. I say this because the government does not have enough internal resources of urban planners and architects who will think more holistically. So, like many other activities, which lack vision, this will also become a piecemeal effort and be left to organic intervention to take its final outcome, forever changing character with time.

The sheer scale of Phase II revamp is daunting, and it will involve several heritage and environmental clearances within the area covering Chhatrapati Shivaji Terminus (CST) to Nariman Point. Makeovers of this scale will need some rigorous planning and implementation of skilled and knowledgeable team.

Architect Ratan Batliboi, who designed the Marine Drive makeover, opines that the project's second phase will further beautify the stretch although he is perplexed as to why the delay persists from the government.

If the upgrade of this stretch is kept simple and its originality is maintained along with restoring heritage buildings, the space will be naturally appealing as opposed to an attempt to mimic a misunderstood imported aspiration. We possibly cannot erase history cosmetically but we can certainly learn to live gracefully with it.

Sabarmati River Front Development

Most urban developments ideally anchor on one central idea of a public space that is ecologically or economically driven, around which subsequent developments spin off, setting the rhythm of what may arrive. Mumbai is devoid of such centrally thought out single anchor and thus it gives you multiple, scattered and non-cohesive entities in urban forms. Sabarmati River Front Development in Ahmedabad, Gujarat, is in sharp contrast in what is happening (or rather not happening) in Mumbai's urban development. I had the opportunity to learn about Dr. Bimal Patel's Sabarmati River Front work during World Architecture Day in Mumbai. It appears socially relevant and inclusive which is evident from several examples he showed of completed work and what he envisages in time to come.

River Sabarmati is important to the city's urban ecology and it has been long acknowledged that appropriate development of the riverfront can turn the river into a major asset; improving the quality of environment, ecology and life in Ahmedabad.

Sabarmati River Front in Ahmedabad, Gujarat (Designed by HCP Design Planning and Management Pvt. Ltd.)

Source: World Architecture News, online. November 2012

The Environmental Planning Collaborative (EPC) was commissioned to prepare a comprehensive feasibility study to develop a 9 km stretch of the city's riverfront. EPC provided development management services to Sabarmati River Front Development Corporation Limited (SRFDCL) until 2002. During this period its mandate was to direct and monitor all the preparatory work. Since then HCP Design Planning and Management Pvt. Ltd. (HCPDPM), headed by Bimal Patel, has been responsible for the project's urban design, master plan and architectural design.

Public spaces cannot be privatized. Public spaces cannot be exclusive.

Thus Sabarmati River Front Project, due to its very nature and aspiration, remains a multi-dimensional public asset, which will not only create a thriving citizen-centric network of parks, promenades, bazaars, and cultural hub, but also work as a structure that will ecologically enhance the city and its resident's relationship to the river. It is one of the most robust urban renewal project that India is witnessing, keeping context and local culture intact without walking all over it.

Sabarmati River Front in Ahmedabad, Gujarat (Designed by HCP Design Planning and Management Pvt. Ltd.)

The ongoing process of the project is premised on these following steps: first, it is to reclaim land, cleaning up existing contamination flowing in to the river and then on to building flood protection wall and laying grid of sewage interceptors that will prevent any further contamination. The sewage lines will carry untreated mass to an augmented treatment plant. Slum dwellers in the area have been relocated to communities of modest housing.

Next, the project provided 11.5 km long pedestrian promenade at the edge along the banks of the river. The promenade is very well connected to proposed streets with wide sidewalks inclusive of bicycle paths which both encourage walking and cycling.

Ongoing and future work includes culture centre, museums, sports facilities, trade fair grounds and open air markets. All of this will enhance Ahmedabad's local living conditions for residents and experience of tourists. The simple joy of being able to walk along the river bank, to sit in a garden and enjoy the serene beauty of the river is now a reality through Sabarmati River Front. The project is currently ongoing, but several parts of the projects are open and being used by the public and the reclaimed space is home to events such as the kite festival.

Transformation through urban renewal in a cohesive manner is possible and probably the only way forward to avoid fragmentation and isolated growth. Communities can thrive and benefit from inspirational projects like Sabarmati River Front and that is the lesson Mumbai cannot be oblivious to.

Project details:

Client: Sabarmati River Front Development Corporation Ltd., Ahmedabad

Site area: 200 hectares

Year of completion: 1997 – Ongoing

Bollywood's Walk of the Stars in Bandra

Circa 2004, tryst with Los Angeles via a road trip. Hollywood's Walk of Fame on Sunset Boulevard was high on our student-tourist mind. Movie star names embedded in five-point pink terrazzo stars rimmed with brass lines inset in dark grey terrazzo tiles. Mumbai has followed Hollywood's footsteps in conceptual idea now and come up with its very own Walk of the Bollywood Stars at Bandra Promenade. It had all the ingredients of Hollywood déjà vu for me. Unfortunately, it didn't feel the same.

The Walk of the Stars opened in March 2012 is a replica concept and bears handprints and signatures of Bollywood stars which are embossed in brass base plates along the promenade. This feature runs about 2.5 km in stretch. The Walk of Stars in Bandra will also feature few statues of Bollywood legends, which will be life-size, perched on one end of the metal benches. That way, die-hard fans can have privilege of getting a picture of themselves sitting next to their worshipped star.

Hollywood's Walk of Fame was a brainchild of E. M. Stuart, volunteer President of Hollywood Chambers of Commerce, in the year 1953. In that sense, Bollywood's almost similarly replicated concept lacks innovation and originality. Times are different, movie fans affection and taste towards Bollywood is evolving, and their perceived sense of public spaces is different. Bollywood itself is evolving and trying hard to reinstate itself for its more sophisticated audience. Then what gave it away to just reproduce a concept almost identical to Hollywood?

Imported concepts in built environment, out of context to its users, are a precarious phenomenon. In India, our sense of public spaces and the way we treat and consume them is quite different from how it might be elsewhere. Our sense of public habits, reaction to trash and maintenance and management, public safety is at a different point on the spectrum compared with other countries.

Source: World Architecture News, online. April 2012

That said, the Walk of the Stars being built as a public space will be free of cost (although heavily guarded for now) and aspires to add value to the promenade. Several Bollywood stars currently reside in the neighbourhood – the most iconic of them being Shah Rukh Khan. In India, Bollywood stars are idolized to a disproportionate level and many people travel from far to just get a glimpse of them. In that sense, it will serve as an open museum of sorts to humanize Bollywood stars, and it might add a layer of imagined proximity of personal connection through hand prints and signatures of the stars they look up to. Something akin to what social media like twitter has done for stars and its fans – more reachable and hence less fantasized.

Chapter 5

Review of old and new buildings and interior spaces

The Capital Building, Mumbai

Capital Building I

Source: World Architecture News, online. January 2012

Capital Building 2

It's a James Law building – James Law of Cybertecture. Architecture and construction industry in Mumbai is currently abuzz with the development of this newest addition. It is none other than the iconic architectural addition aptly called "The Capital". It is centrally located in the Bandra–Kurla Complex (BKC), a rapidly growing business district in Mumbai. This futuristic commercial building aims to house some of the most prestigious and prominent international corporations and banks.

The building integrates two key components: revolutionary design and sustainability. The front facade of the building encloses an inset egg-shaped feature, which will house LED panels, which will not only play as a dynamic information display but also act as a functional shading device for the building's front yard. With premium amenities like smart parking and sky lobby, the building offers tenants an office space of AAA-rating. Along with world-class amenities and finishes, the building also integrates sustainability with several energy-efficient strategies. Use of light diffusers reflecting natural light in common areas will reduce the demand on lighting energy and floor plates are equipped with operable windows, which will enable individual tenants with natural ventilation for healthy and sustainable built spaces. The design also incorporates naturalistic waterfalls and internally vegetated areas to cool the building naturally from within. This will reduce the HVAC load, effectively reducing the demand on overall energy consumption. The building uses cladding system with Polyvinylidene Fluoride (PVDF) coating, which is a sturdy finish with respect to weathering and ultra-violet degradation. This will further add to the energy savings in the building.

In addition to its innovative design and energy-efficient strategies, the building offers another advantage – its enviable location at the Bandra–Kurla Complex. BKC is giving Nariman Point, once an only premium business district located in South Mumbai, a run for its money. With central location, accessibility and rapid upscale development, BKC has positioned itself as the sought-after location for businesses.

The Capital building is nearing completion and with about 80% complete, the building is expected to be commissioned in the first quarter of 2012. Construction of the building began circa 2008 and with possible completion in the year 2012; it is an impressive pace for a project of this scale.

The Capital building will elevate corporate real estate quality by another degree and thus push the envelope in built environment in Mumbai and will be a sophisticated neighbour to existing buildings like ICICI bank and Infrastructure Leasing & Financial Services Limited (IL&FS) building.

Agastya Office Development in Kurla

Sometime ago, an architect had asked me, "if one has to go look at significant architectural work in the city, which are the buildings one should keep in mind?" I was blank for a long time and I couldn't think of anything worth mentioning with the exception of older part of town in Fort and Colaba. I don't know if this is a good thing for an aspirational city like Mumbai? With the surge of Bandra–Kurla Complex (BKC), one does get hopeful though. There is hope in its potential.

Bandra–Kurla Complex

With BKC being the newer central business district, it has affected the surrounding locations significantly. Once, not-so popular destinations like Kurla are getting a boost through new developments. Agastya Office Development designed by London-based architects Foster+Partners will transform this one part of industrial belt into a

Source: World Architecture News, online. July 2012

corporate office development.The project comprises of five buildings, of three to seven storeys, along with a sequence of terraced roof gardens. It is such a welcome relief to see something horizontal than the typical vertical glass developments. Moreover, it's an expansive development, which has wonderfully avoided the usual tall and dense kind.

The office accommodation is aimed to be flexible – its 18-m-wide floor plates have the potential to accommodate trading floors, an open-plan IT office, which can be adapted for singular offices at the perimeter or centre of each floor. Below the bands of vision glazing on each floor, a ventilation duct and a storage area is projected to create a bull-nose façade detail, clad in reflective stainless steel.

The green building strategies in Agastya Office Development include combination of high levels of natural daylight with external shading and a ventilation strategy that minimizes the need for suspended ceilings ensuring healthier indoor air quality for occupants. The environmental strategies included are green roofs which will absorb rainwater and grey water to be recycled, further reducing water consumption by around 50 percent.Together, these measures will help to set new standards for energy.

The project is under construction, and remains a significant design by Foster+Partners, in a city, which is witnessing mediocre glass buildings addition at a rapid rate.

Bharat Diamond Bourse: Bandra–Kurla Complex (BKC)

Architecture is a perception to our faculties. It can be felt associatively or empathetically which essentially means you can either deconstruct it intellectually or emotionally but never remain detached. I am going to attempt explaining these words in coming paragraphs.

Bharat Diamond Bourse (BDB) was set up with the objective of establishing necessary infrastructural facilities for promotion of export of diamonds including diamond jewelry from India eventually making India an International Trading Centre for gems and jewelry. The mixed-use development to accomplish this is about to get completed at BKC. The Bourse Complex is spread over an area of 20 acres. The total constructed area is 2 million sq ft and the development consists of 8 buildings of 9 floors.

By and large, this expansive development remains monotonous and instantly instills a sense of industrial boredom every time I have pass by and I think about the fatigued and insipid effort that has gone behind it and wonder, what gives?

Serenity and banality are two different things in architecture. In BDB, it is pure banality that has overtaken and can be easily misunderstood as harmony of order. But there is a visual discomfort in its collective presence.

Large glass façade of BDB, intermittently broken with slightly taller towers do not exude grace. Building's average lifespan stretches for 50–60 years and, unlike a work of art or literature that we don't like, we may well see a work of architecture every day, whether they serve as a background or foreground to the skyline.

BKC's skyline is a nascent one, so there isn't much scope to ruminate over what the aspirations of this business district are. Development pace allows newer styles and materials to seep in, in building styles. Buildings are inherently expected to remain timeless during their lifetime with respect to style and justify their presence in more convincing ways.

Source: World Architecture News, online. June 2012

In that sense, BDB strikes as a morose mechanical development and much remains to be desired and the truth is that it is and now alive and we have to live with it for few decades. It can't be undone, not in near future. That is the fate architecture presents you with.

So far, BKC skyline leaves much to be explored from architectural perspective. Till date, one that stands in my mind is *Platina* building, despite it being slightly old; its play with location, sense of geometry and proportion still communicates elegance, which its newest immediate neighbouring building *Sofitel* has failed quite miserably. This proves to me that elegance and timelessness in buildings are quite detached with rapid technological advances. Even if we consider the latest building the *Capital* and compare it to *Platina*, much remains to be desired from the *Capital*. It sure is grand and dramatic but leaves me feeling empty. Future may hold a more dramatic and vanity-driven building, and it may render the Capital glass box majesty trailing.

Coming back to BDB, it has lessons in its making. Large doesn't mean it should have been thoughtless, and expansive doesn't mean it should have been lifeless. For now it remains, a study of a part that belongs to a larger scheme of things of upcoming Bandra–Kurla Complex, of what is working and what is not.

Ellipsis Restaurant opens in Colaba

Colaba gets it again. Somehow, the old charm of Colaba continues to attract new additions of restaurants and clubs. Old heritage buildings retain their charm and exude a sense of timelessness by keeping the high-profile new businesses coming in.Amarchand Mansion on Madame Cama Road is now home to a swanky and expensive restaurant, Ellipsis.

Designed by award-winning German designer Thomas Schoos of California, USA, Ellipsis stays true to its belonging of 19th century building. Schoos's basic play with the original underlying elements of colonial era is noteworthy. Features are not covered and hidden with contemporary materials. By doing so and yet creating a new look that fuses past with the new must have been an interesting challenge that Schoos must have loved to take on. He has managed this quite successfully.

Keeping old elements intact as much as possible, along with introducing new design features which are subtle and yet blend effortlessly is not easy. What Thomas Schoos has done is played with subtleties and introduced carefully crafted understated furniture assortment, light fixtures, wooden flooring and soft furnishings at places. Overall impact is downplayed but still comes together as striking in its own way. For a designer, this is an achievement.

Schoos has played a lot with walls, accent lighting and brought in a splash of vintage paintings; and they have been placed randomly that makes one feel, as if you're touring a painter's house with a sneak peek of his personal space and work.

Ellipsis is an upscale place, which aims to cater to crème de la crème people of the town. This is an elite expensive restaurant by all standards. The owners Rohan Talwar and Ranbir Batra have spared no expense to compromise on the experience they intended to create. Bespoke built environment to carefully crafted menu of food and drinks and detailed attention to staff training, their designer uniforms, all aiming to constitute an experience.

Fine dining is all about creating a unique experience through not just food but also a complete spatial experience where people like to keep coming back for a slice of that exquisite and exceptional savoir-faire.

Source: World Architecture News, online. June 2012

Surge of façade designing in built environment

Architecture constantly evolves in response to forces in technology, sustainability, politics and culture of a given country and to its prevailing dynamics. Previously, architects designed the whole building and scope of their services encompassed designing the complete building. I am seeing a change in this phenomenon of having different specialized built environment professionals to design façade of buildings in the city of Mumbai. As buildings get more sophisticated, there is an encumbrance to design them more efficiently to respond to technological and sustainable needs of the times.

Façade designers incorporate creativity and engineering to optimize to best respond to project needs. They carefully consider each building for its historical significance, local climatic conditions and design engineer the envelope and façade, thus offering best of material suggestions, thermal modelling, efficiency and optimized design which gives best of the front access and minimize building maintenance once the building is completed and occupied.

Mumbai is seeing considerable rise in demand for upgraded buildings, which are not just glossy but include intrinsic efficiency offered for its owners and tenants. Thus, in a high-end project, demand to incorporate sophisticated technology is being adopted by many builders and developers. And rightly so. In a long run, if this ensures building's longevity and improved healthy built environment to its inhabitants, it's worth the extra investment.

TCG Financial Center by the Chatterjee Group located at Bandra–Kurla Complex is one such example. This commercial building is now complete and had its façade design done by Gregory H. Romine led Axis Façade Group. Axis Façade specializes in façade design and have done extensive work all across the world. They have done extensive work in India as Façade Designers, especially in Delhi and Mumbai.

Source: World Architecture News, online. May 2012

For TCG Financial Center, they were engaged for material applications, schematic design, design development, construction documents, unit cost estimate, quantity survey, procurement and construction administration for all façade elements including unitized curtain wall, glass vertical sunshades, metal cladding, integrated lighting and BMU/façade access design. The project features a horizontal pattern offset with vertical glass and embedded high definition metallic sunshades. Lighting is integrated into the curtain wall to enhance the stature of the building during the evening hours.

With that, façade design makes a stronger case and urges builders and developers to factor in lifecycle cost incurred in using improved engineered buildings methodologies. If built environments offer better value on investment through improved healthier and efficient spaces, then it is not only cost effective but also saves hidden costs incurred while using inefficiently designed buildings through health perils, energy maintenance costs.

Google opens its Mumbai office

Google has been sort of a beacon of change with respect to Internet and pioneered in many ways to revolutionize the way Internet was used for information. Somehow, that level of innovation completely misses from the workplaces they provide for their employees. Google has always projected their office environments as a creative amalgam of fun and innovation. I, as a design professional, have never quite agreed to their 'fun place to work for' message. Simply because fun is not that simplistic, which may not be achieved just by providing a pool table and colourful bean bags, so to speak. Mature built environments, especially for offices usually stay away from thematic representation. This is primarily because spending extensive time in such environments can be tiresome to the psyche and induced fun, like Google is attempting can have varied reaction from person to person.

Google's Mumbai new office is a classic case of cultural elements kitsch, that too taken bit literally. In this case, it has taken all the possible Mumbai stereotypes that one can think of superficially and put them together in even more hackneyed, non-clever format. Bright colours, kite flying, Cricket, Dabbawaalas, Bollywood, Indian fabrics, all put together, which appears to be a hurried design attempt, that too, in an unsophisticated format.

Thematic representations may work for restaurants or spaces where one is not spending extensive amounts of time. Themes work better when you want to create a drama for an experience. Designed dramatic spaces and experience in small doses work well. I wonder how one will not get weary of the childlike theme in an office environment, where one spends large amount of time of their day?

Enduring, carefully crafted built spaces are achieved through mature consideration, experience and deeper understanding of how people work, behave and consume spaces. This goes for carefully crafted fun spaces as well. How productivity and creativity can be triggered in workspaces is a matter of deliberations over several

Source: World Architecture News, online. May 2012

factors on nature of work, interaction patterns amongst employees, company's culture, employee's culture and the desired outcome. To put matters in perspective, it's a clear case of behavioural science and how well it can be applied to workspaces.

Fun is also a lot inwardly gazing. No amount of bright colours and fun motifs will trigger fun in mind if one is thinking of solving a serious work problem or simply distracted. Won't such a place create mental environmental noise constantly, hindering thought pattern? Moreover, this assumes that all the employees who will work here will come with same frame of mind, identical conditioning, looking for equally fun work environment with exactly what Google defines as 'fun'.

Hermès Store comes to Fort, Mumbai

Hermès, a French luxury brand, opened its shop in Mumbai recently. It is quietly perched in the lanes of Fort near Horniman Circle. The building that houses Hermès store is unassuming, yet announces softly its Victorian period belonging. And thus cleverly announces that the store has adaptive re-use of interior built space which has been more common in areas like Fort and Colaba of Mumbai with buildings of Victorian era.

Parisian architectural design firm RDAI, founded by Rena Dumas and directed by Denis Montel, has designed the store. The store's quaint location and subdued exterior treatment set an exclusivity mood for its shoppers. Arched entry way has been maintained from the original building and sets the tone for an unadulterated retail experience that is about to begin.

The store is spread over 3,000 sq ft and split on two levels. A stone-cladded staircase that wraps itself around a glass elevator achieves a point of focus – thus connecting the two floors, such that two levels appear as one. The designers have used ample wood and mosaic flooring throughout the store. But there is a difference. All the materials exude clean lines, non-fussy treatment, making it remarkable by its richness.

Mosaic flooring in white, grey and red showcase a traditional 24 Faubourg Saint-Honoré motifs. Demarcation of spaces remains low-energy and non-descript with subtle white walls and furniture pieces that are simply cut and linear in their presence. Spaces are cleverly dotted with accent leather furniture pieces, designed by Rena Dumas, just to add appropriate amount of focal points that seamlessly fit into the entire light look of the sophisticated store. Similar kind of feel is carried forward upstairs as well. Warmth of wooden parquet flooring and tall white ceilings with accentuated lighting played perfectly to enhance the merchandise. Such non-daunting retail environments add to the experience without being overbearing and highlight just about what needs to play up.

Source: World Architecture News, online. March 2012

Hermès give a sense of being large in scale, being subtly dramatic yet never loses its feel of warmth and coziness throughout the store making an ideal statement what the brand stands for and what it has in store for the shoppers looking for something exclusive and quality driven.

For what it's worth, retail interior environments in India are still at a nascent stage but that is changing every minute as we speak. With more and more foreign brands entering the Indian terrain and local brands upping their game, it offers an interesting mix to study retail branding and environments. It will rise tremendously in coming years and shift of shopping from need-based to experience-based paradigm is not far for India. Examples like Hermès store in Mumbai highlight this shift well for us to investigate.

Team: Artistic Director Denis Montel | **Project Interior Architect,** Véronique Duchesne

Imperial Tower by Adrian Smith+ Gordon Gill

News of Imperial Tower Competition was out in first week of May 2013. It has been bagged by Adrian Smith+ Gordon Gill of Chicago, same team that designed Burj Khalifa in Dubai. Although, the project is on hold as per AS+GG until further news release. Imperial Tower in Mumbai is set to be the tallest residential tower, with 116 stories and 400 m tall. And that sounds splendid and egoistic in aspiration but conflicted in context of extreme conditions. It often made me wonder that how did our egos turn so fragile?

But then cities like Mumbai never poised themselves on humanitarian grounds. It's a city of aggressive entrepreneurship, capitalistic in spirit with heady rush not usually found, so far, in any other city in India. It conflates this conflicted human spirit of dualism and that is remarkably evident in its architectural aspirations.

The Imperial Tower is poised as a softer yet taller, much taller in height and it is said to minimize the negative effects of wind. There are sky gardens with access to natural light, views and connection to Arabian Sea like never before. The tower will offer one of the most spacious and luxurious residences in Mumbai. The 76,272 sq m tower includes 132 residential units between 195 and 1,115 sq m, along with serviced apartments between 72 and 252 sq m. It's a project with superlative adjectives in built environment.

According to the news brief from AS+GG, the Imperial Tower will aim at highest form of sustainability with rainwater harvesting, high-efficiency mechanical systems and green-wall podium landscape with native plants.

Looking at the juxtaposed impressions of the Imperial Tower to the existing neighborhood buildings, there is something contrarian in their styles. They do not give you a unifying feeling, just like the city they belong to. Buildings don't talk to each other or to the site. Once, such varied aspirations take shape in the Mumbai skyline, I wonder if its schism will be of a concern to the city and its people? Or the magic of token rise in building heights will be sufficient for now and in the future?

Source: World Architecture News, online. May 2013

Le Mill Lifestyle Store: A case study for adaptive reuse project

Source: World Architecture News, online. April 2012

Le Mill, one of Mumbai's multifunctional lifestyle concept store, opened few months ago. Le Mill is housed in a former rice mill right in the middle of the city's tenacious dock area covering 15,000 sq ft converted into a store. It is a clever adaptive reuse project, which has been popular in Mumbai's former mill buildings. When old buildings become unsuitable for their programmatic intentions, as progress in technology, politics and economics restructures itself faster than the built environment; adaptive reuse becomes a sustainable option for the reclamation of sites with more affordability.

Founders Cecilia Morelli Parikh, Julie Leymarie, Aurelie de Limlette, and Le Mill's fashion consultant Anaita Shroff Adajania are passionate about creating an atmosphere where customers will want to spend time and just hang out and browse through experience that is on the racks.

The store houses an expansive feel; the finishes are neat with rustic to less-finished, complementing a very contemporary ambience. By including an organic cafe, a flower shop and a book section, the owners hope to foster a laid-back social atmosphere without the pressure of amounting to a retail purchase obligation. Much appreciated.

Architect Ashiesh Shah who designed this space has stayed true to the original vision of the owners of keeping it as a space where people can spend time without assumed restriction. He has played with levels, dividing and demarcating to create multiple sections. This allows the experience to be explorative in an unintentional way. There are no rigid signages. You explore as you go and stumble on nooks and sections stocked with variety of things with playful lighting. Serendipity!

Coming back to adaptive reuse, the designer has kept the structural additions to a minimum and maintained rafters and high ceilings from the original building. The industrial feel is completed with exposed

HVAC ducts and ceiling hung light fixtures. It adds drama and we do away with an additional layer of false ceiling. Flooring is exposed concrete with just a hint of gloss using semi-finished polish. Its un-completeness makes a statement, a positive one.

Most striking feature of this store is the vivacious use of visual merchandising elements. Wire hung merchandise from the ceiling, lavishly spread in a whitewashed wall background, and corrugated sheets and semi-finished wooden crates panels. Put together, they create drama with effective use of mood lighting. Le Mill makes for a noteworthy adaptive reuse projects.

Mill conversion or adaptive reuse, a process whereby a usually historic mill or industrial / factory building is restored or rehabilitated into another use such as residential housing, retail shops, offices, or a mix of non-industrial elements. These conversions have been quite popular in Mumbai with such projects usually located in the central part of Mumbai, Lower Parel, where multiple decommissioned mill sites still exist.

Per-forma Studio's The Great Eastern Hotel

Per-forma Studio, a New York based architecture practice run by an architect, Sarika Bajoria, has recently been garnering attention for all the right reasons. The practice started in 2010 and remains young! I anticipate better amalgamation of 'East and West' sensibilities (if there is a distinction between the two). India's case is new and its challenges unique and thus there has to be greater importance towards contextual architectural aspirations. Not to mention, these are exhilarating times for India and we will see a great deal of stimulating, disturbing, provocative and promising built spaces. Indian sensibilities have never been ruffled to this extent and it's not necessarily a bad thing. This fertile time can be a great period of reinvention in terms of architecture. Thus, practices like Per-Forma Studio who have exposure to more than one country are expected to go beyond narrow vision of architecture and push the envelope of excellence.

Per-forma Studio is currently embarked on designing a mixed-use development called The Great Eastern which is spread over 8.6 acres of previously textile mill land located in the heart of Mumbai. The development will include retail, hospitality, lifestyle and entertainment spaces. The conceptual design of the hotel is out and the design attempts to bring in 'spinning and weaving' – the site's original purpose of textile mill.

This 8.6 acres development is split in two phases. The first phase includes 2.2 acres mixed-use development of overall area that spans 6 lakh sq ft. In addition to the hotel, the development will also include a clubhouse, high-end retail, restaurants, cafés, and spa, sort of giving it a holistic spin.

The form of the hotel is undulating and organic. As Sarika says, 'the intertwining of the new and old, modern amenities and sanctity of undisturbed nature, relaxation, shopping, entertainment and luxury within the design creates a unique visual and holistic experience.'

Source: World Architecture News, online. February 2013

She further explains, 'a strategy of analyzing solar radiation performance in conjunction with developing building information modeling system was adopted to develop an intelligent and sustainable facade solution that responds to solar heat gain and visibility. Sun insolation analysis data informed the shift in WWR (window wall ratios) of the façade.'

This brings me to the point that has constantly troubled me about Mumbai as a built environment professional. These attempts of creating islands of sanitized developments, however serious, where most of the mixed-use are attempted in such a way that the sum of all pieces gives a fragmented understanding to a holistic city precincts at best. Moving forward, I haven't seen a larger public dialogue on this issue amongst urban design fraternity and government authorities. This is worrisome to a large extent because Mumbai is still not serious to propose a relevant big picture of master plan of the city. Thus, it would be unfair to put the burden only on architects and designers to reform complex political and economic realms through architectural aspirations alone.

Newest shoppers' destination: Phoenix Market City Mall

The latest (partially complete) mixed-used development is located a little east of Bandra–Kurla Complex in Mumbai. Phoenix Market City, spread over 25 acres, located on LBS Marg, will have massive 42 lakh sq ft of built area in phases. The development, which primarily includes retail outlets, will house office buildings, a premium hotel, outdoor courtyards, entertainment areas and community spaces like serviced apartments. Given its holistic approach, the project has generated good amount of interest among real estate professionals. Moreover, the location of this development is strategic: close to BKC, the newer commercial district of Mumbai.

Phoenix Market City I

That being said, the focus of this essay is the month-old shopping landmark, Phoenix Market City (PMC). It is one the largest and the biggest malls in Mumbai and as much as it is expansive; it is about

Source: World Architecture News, online. January 2012

housing exclusive brands and flagship stores. PMC brings about 330 international brands in apparel, jewellery, footwear, food & beverage and much more. If successful, *Mumbaites* will not be rushing to Dubai, Bangkok or Singapore for their international shopping experience and brand quotient. The mall will serve as an international hub of retail outlets for enthusiastic shoppers. Zara, Nike and Puma with their flagship stores and CEX, L'Occitane, Luxury Boulevard, Café Pico making their first entry in India and with BEBE, AND, Vero Moda, FCUK and with many more, the mall will be a much sought-after retreat for shoppers. It will serve as an ultimate consumerist destination; all combined under one roof.

Phoenix Market City 2

The mall aims at providing its visitors an enhanced service, a complete experience of shopping and will offer concierge service, home delivery, one point bookings, valet parking, child-care and fashion consultants in addition to access to brands from world over. The mall is determined to redefine lifestyle by bringing a highly upgraded and integrated shopping experience. The mall houses eight movie screens, gold lounges (capable of hosting film festivals) and multiple dining options with variety of cuisines.

For a commercial project, certain consumption percentage has to be met for businesses to be profitable. Indians have inherently not been brand consumerist in nature and that could also be because it was never before available to them at this scale along with their rising disposable incomes. As Paco Underhill, author of *Why We Buy:* The Science of Shopping points out, "Customers in India are missing better prices. Customers are missing a better experience in the store". Factors like traditions, culture and evolving value system will all play a role here. Like any other developing nation in the world, Indians are getting more and more brand conscious and economically this is enabling them to experiment to find their transforming identity. How it will play up in coming years to redefine their uniqueness is still a mystery. Whether they will turn into a homogenized version of their western counterparts or restate their hybrid identity will be interesting to observe in the coming years.

Historical Rajabai Clock Tower scheduled for restoration

The Fort, Mumbai campus of University of Mumbai, houses a clock tower built in the Victorian era and took its iconic form in the precinct just around the onset of the British Raj. The Rajabai Clock Tower was designed by an English architect, George Gilbert Scott. And by no surprise, he had fashioned it roughly around the Big Ben, the Clock Tower of Palace of Westminster in UK. The total cost of construction was INR 2 lakhs a hefty sum for the era it was built in. This entire cost was borne by Premchand Roychand, a prosperous broker who founded the Bombay Stock Exchange on the condition that the tower be named after his mother Rajabai. The tower was built with Malad and Porbandar stone using Burmese teakwood.

As for many historic buildings in Colaba and Fort area of Bombay, Rajabai Tower was too denied preservation and conservation efforts in the past. Some conservation architects and activists have long fought this battle to preserve this part of physical history and have demanded attention through maintenance. Unfortunately, for progressive India, history is of less importance.

However, even though conservation architects are in minority, this hasn't given them a reason to fizzle out their battle. So, with a bit of patience, funds have been raised to meet the estimated budget of restoration of INR 4.2 crores donated by Tata Consultancy Services of India. Curious thing to note here is that the funding raised is through a private corporation and not from public funds. Government seems to be always missing from important civic projects.

Architecture firm, Somaya and Kalappa of Mumbai, have been chosen to carry out this work. The firm, led by architect Brinda Somaya, has been at the forefront in advocacy of restoration of historic built environments across India.

The plan of the commissioned work has not been made public yet. But news is that the scope of work will include a thorough cleaning of the façade, repair and/or replacement of damaged exterior stone,

Source: World Architecture News, online. May 2012

structural strengthening, stopping of water leakage, removal of plants and biological growth, refurbishment of the Burma teakwood fittings in the library, provision of services like wiring and air-conditioning where they are needed, and facilities to help preserve rare books in the library's collection. The work on Rajabai Tower restoration is awaiting two things, required approvals from city officials and the monsoon season to pass.

Work is expected to begin right after both are taken care of and is expected to be completed in 2 years time.

Amen to that!

Giorgio Armani to design Signature Residences at World One

Luxury knows no upper limit – which is increasingly becoming the case in Mumbai's high-end residential sector with developers eyeing mostly the crème de la crème customers. There is a race to outdo every preceding style and expense on a built project like never before. With that said, Mumbai's World One Towers coming up at Worli will be world's tallest residential tower comprising of 117 floors.

The World One Towers will have exclusive three and four bedroom World Residences, lavish World Villas with a private pool, and the luxurious duplex World Mansions with private pool, gym and personal elevator. They will flaunt a price tag of INR 10 crores to 50 crores. With that kind of pricing, there will be a rigorous screening process for interested buyers to be qualified to afford affluence of this magnitude. Criteria to be qualified for such provincial exclusivity are unknown at best or not under the purview of public knowledge in India.

Giorgio Armani's design studio, known as Armani/Casa, has been designing the interiors of these residences. The studio is known to work only with most discerning exclusive clientele and as such will have luxury that creates bespoke living spaces. Giorgio Armani, president and chief executive officer of the Giorgio Armani Group, who also designed residences, Burj Khalifa in Dubai, says that the World Towers is an all-encompassing undertaking that transforms the notions of architecture and technology, and is geared to create a new and unprecedented aesthetic experience. When probed further about how Armani brand fits into the traditions and culture that have been critical to Indian history, he explains that "traditions and culture have become widely assimilated into general work culture" and that he is attempting to respect and integrate that incredible history fusing with his own design aesthetics. The designer from Armani also reveal that the group has finalised on opening the first retail outlet of Armani-branded furnishings, tiles and bathroom fittings among other

Source: World Architecture News, online. February 2012

things in Mumbai. The first shipment is expected in the next four to six months.

Armani explains that he has introduced elements to reference the project's country location: so there is fretwork, craftsmanship and detailing, with metallic reflections of white gold leaf, liquid metal and special wall finishes.

Real estate experts have voiced their concerns that viable appetite for such luxury living is nearly missing with lack of high-level job creations with salaries of this magnitude, which may enable potential homeowners to buy houses that appear astronomical. Huge class divide is not an alien feature to Mumbai and somehow there is a strange kind of muted comfort with two worlds, which cannot be more different yet passively forced to co-exist. And projects like these further tip the scale of inequality although creating an ephemeral sense of fabricated exuberance.

Bombay Arts Society, Bandra

As soon as you swirl left from Bandra–Worli Sea Link, there is a mud brown coloured, asymmetrical, softly curved new building in the

Bombay Arts Society 001

Source: World Architecture News, online. August 2013

foreground of Lilavati Hospital. This building, ingeniously simple and persuasive in its presence, is none other than Bombay Arts Society, housed right opposite Rang Sharda in Bandra. As you approach the building, it's surrounded by openness and swaying trees in a quaint setting of Bandra. It makes for an appealing background for the building as long as you avoid looking directly at the pile of garbage on either side of the building plot.

Bombay Arts Society 002

There is something special about this project, as it is one of the first buildings in Mumbai, which is truly meant as a public facility. It is aimed to serve the arts and the artist community in a non-exclusive manner. This is impressive and hopefully will pave way for many more public facilities similar to public libraries open to all residents of Mumbai. The decision to have a centre for artists that was easily accessible from the Mumbai suburbs was made a few years ago and that is when the plans for this project in Bandra began.

Bombay Arts Society stands on an extremely small plot of 1,300 sq m and is aimed as a mixed-use building. The building houses an art gallery, a small auditorium, a cafeteria and artist rooms, which were all incorporated in 1,000 sq m of space. As you enter the building there is a swaying reception to your right with a curvilinear staircase in the backdrop. And spaces that it leads to on the following floors are all organic and softly punctuated to inherit the curved exterior form of the building. This merges well with what building's architect Sanjay Puri said in his interview: "The fluidity of form seen externally, with a concrete skin encapsulating spaces while undulating in both the horizontal and vertical planes, is carried through to the interior volumes making the entire experience as that of moving through a sculpture". Indeed, the building appears a lot like a soft sculpture in form yet somehow remains understated with its colour and exterior material, which feels very empowering in a subtle way.

Bombay Arts Society 003

The building, which people often tell the architect, resembles Henri Moore's cubist sculptures. To create an illusionary sense of space, architect Sanjay Puri used a wire mesh for the structure of the building as well as floating columns. Hence, there are no straight columns that run directly from the top to bottom of the building.

This is clearly evidenced in the interior spaces which are free of corners and only have fluidity and merging of curves.

After almost 3 years, the Bombay Arts Society building is now getting ready to open its doors to the public in a month's timeframe. Established nearly 122 years ago, the Bombay Art Society so far was based in Jehangir Art Gallery and has been serving art and artists ever since. Hence, to have a more centrally located facility in the city is a welcome move. Bandra continues to prove its central location as something of a strategic benefit which the linear city could hinge its development on.

Architect Sanjay Puri's design philosophy is simple and fluid as evident in this project. It stands distinct in form and stature unlike any other building that he has designed in the past. Perhaps, like he says, design 'for' and 'within' the context is important. That said, yes, context is important and is often repeated by practitioners, although I continue to remain befuddled, as I do not know what the true architectural context of Mumbai is anymore. Old colonial remains, newer changes wanting to surface in built environment or half way between old and new or neither? These questions may not present comfortable answers that work holistically to the entire city and its aspirations.

For now on, we should find glory in getting this new building for creative blood in the city and proclaim the idea of public spaces wholeheartedly that truly belong to people. The Bombay Arts Society building is a welcome step in that direction.

Biomimicry as a guiding force to design Lavasa township

Settled in a picturesque land and spread over 12,500 acres is a town of Lavasa which is about 2 hours drive from Mumbai. It is a town that is soon becoming a planned destination where visitors would throng in large numbers. HOK International has worked on the township planning with Biomimicry as their guiding principle to design this expansive development. Working closely with biologists from Biomimicry 3.8, HOK International has spearheaded this effort and done extensive study of the local ecosystem and devised strategies that work in harmony with local biome as well as climatology. The team at HOK developed an overall master plan for the town and coupled it with landscape design to minimize deforestation and have a future progressive environment-friendly landscape performance plan in tow.

The development is expected to complete in the year 2020 which will include 5 planned urban villages that can accommodate a population of 30–50 thousand people. The planning team has made conscious effort to integrate local traditional principles of planning and tie it with indigenous forms of buildings and sustainable built environment as opposed to replicating western model of urban settlements. This development relies heavily on sustainability principles of energy conservation, reduction in demand of natural resources and waste management.

The project has already garnered several awards with the likes of Award of Honour in Analysis and Planning (Dasve Village Master Plan) – American Society of Landscape Architects, for its fresh and holistic approach and giving nature its chance to teach sustainable human settlement through biomimicry.

The importance that sustainability has gained in current times is something all built-environment professionals need to take into account. Mindless hauling and manufacturing to suit our ever-increasing needs has already taken its toll. In an ideal world, there will be no waste and usage of only recyclable materials – as that is how the nature and ecosystem was designed. It's time for us to take a cue from it and design our man-made ecosystem.

Source: World Architecture News, online. February 2013

Chapter 6

Local architecture events on built environment

World Architecture Day, 2012

You will always stumble on inspiration when you least expect it and somehow that inspiration will revive your eroding faith and turn you hopeful again. Unexpectedly, my experience was exactly that, when I attended World Architecture Day last Monday on 8th of October, 2012, here in Mumbai. All the speakers talked about a city of past when Mumbai was Bombay, a city of hope, vibrancy and opportunities which have degraded and somehow hope has gone missing. I came back satisfied and rejuvenated, with an urge to do more.

Mostly all the talks, especially the ones by Professor K.T. Ravindran, Vikas Dilawari, Bimal Patel and Christopher Benninger tackled some of the most basic issues plaguing Indian cities. But they all, through their exemplary work, have tackled these problems head on, fearlessly. They all talked about reincarnation of the city with urban renewal and regeneration.

Dr. Bimal Patel's work on Sabarmati riverfront in Gujarat is etched in my mind. He has changed the paradigm of public space and continues to do so with his exemplary work. It's enduring, inclusive and socially relevant with the context very much in forefront.

Architect Vikas Dilawari's work has been in conservation and preservation of built environment of several communities in Mumbai. And his work, which rightfully has earned him many accolades, is an example of years of persistence and dogged determination.

Architect Christopher Benninger is working closely with Government of Bhutan in creating a feasible urban development plan which will be worth its while in facing forces and challenges in coming years as the country undergoes urbanization. He remained utmost humble, extremely funny and yet profound all the way.

Almost all of them spoke of major issues of decongestion, affordable housing, open spaces, public spaces and inclusive slum rehabilitation while keeping them in context of city reality with respect to rapid urbanization of India.

Source: World Architecture News, online. October 2012

Coming together of architects and built environment fraternity without a commercial aspect attached to it was the first of its kind in Mumbai. There was passion, honesty and only true speaking of their minds. It was truly a celebration of architecture and aspirations that all of us carry and will continue to do so to claim our cities. It was a day to remind that architecture is one of the core professions and architects will remain as key drivers in economic growth, supporting aspirations and nurturing innovation of city dwellers. World Architecture Day left me inspired in more ways than I can explain in words and I hope to carry this message forward to others in days to come.

Hanbury Evans Wright Vlattas + Company visits Mumbai

Hanbury Evans Wright Vlattas + Company, an architecture and planning firm with an unique international expertise in facilities for higher education, based in Virginia, USA, visited Mumbai and Delhi in February 2012, as part of VALET Grant Program. Virginia Leaders in Export Trade (VALET) 2011 grant is an award-winning program overseen by Virginia Economic Development Partnership that assists Virginia firms in expanding and forging international ties through businesses. Through this program, each year, 25 qualifying firms accelerate their marketing efforts in remote countries. The VALET program provides capital resources, along with professional expertise through private-sector partnerships. Post this program, firms have reported an 88 percent increase in international businesses. As part of the program, Hanbury Evans has visited Saudi Arabia twice already and future plans include Brazil, Canada and China with this being their first visit to India.

To bolster their background research, Hanbury Evans began with resources like University World News, which gave an overview of India's purposeful initiative to expand student enrolment by 30 percent in the coming decade. This led to further inquiry into how the Indian education system is structured in ramifications of state, central, autonomous and private universities and how those institutes are gearing up towards growth and improvement. Deborah Marquardt, an associate with Hanbury Evans also began following World Architecture News weekly metro blog on Mumbai which aided her to gauge current architecture and design happenings in the city. In her words, "reading WAN metro blog is almost like reading local design newspaper". She connected with me through metro blog's editor, Sian Disson, to explore if I can assist them in any way in understanding the market better. I was delighted to hear from Sian and consequently connect with Deborah and was keen to meet the firm. To me, Hanbury Evans brings a wealth of knowledge and expertise in a specialized sector of campus and university planning.

Source: World Architecture News, online. February 2012

In my current understanding, Mumbai's construction activities appear to be short-sighted in overall planning and value addition that can be achieved through integrated planning and a holistic vision. And this is where I see, Hanbury Evans visit being timely and invigorating which will hopefully spark interest in comprehensive development of the city creating richer, more meaningful built environments.

I was fortunate to meet the firm's President Jane Cady Wright, FAIA, and Principal, Scott Miller and get to spend some quality time in learning from their rich experience on higher education work with the universities in United States. In my experience, such meetings bring out valuable cross-cultural explorations and insights which are difficult to come by otherwise through available resources. Next morning, both Jane and Scott were keen in touring my undergraduate campus set in heart of the city, before they headed out to Delhi. We went around the campus exploring various buildings and sharing perspectives and capturing images. As Jane kindly puts it, "It was so great to meet 'the face behind the blog'! In planning for our recent trip to Mumbai, WAN's recently launched Metro blogs provided meaningful insight on current architectural happenings in India; however, we were delighted to actually meet Pallavi Shrivastava, WAN's Mumbai blogger. Pallavi graciously met with us and shared her perspective on the architectural community in Mumbai, which greatly enhanced our understanding of the business and design issues of the region".

Tadao Ando's Mumbai visit

Architect Tadao Ando had visited Mumbai a couple of months ago and unfortunately, I had given his lecture a miss. But this event (and visits by architects from outside India) has generated an interesting mix of debate in architectural fraternity here in India. More on this in just a bit.

Tadao Ando is a Japanese architect whose work has been primarily in Japan and carries a distinctive style. He is highly regarded for his extensive contribution in the field of architecture and has bagged several notable awards. His style of creative use of lighting and maintaining natural settings giving Zen-like outcome are hallmarks of his work.

The most unforgettable example that comes to my mind is Church of the Light in Ibaraki, Osaka, Japan. Paul Goldberger, in "Why Architecture Matters", explained it as "a simple rectangle of smooth concrete, sliced through by a freestanding wall set at fifteen-degree angle to the rectangle, as if it were a huge panel that had been swung on hinge". He explains his reaction of being in Church of the Light as something transcending of a spiritual quest. And while experiencing religious buildings, he mentions something profound on the effect that Architecture and built environment can have. "Ultimately this is a space that has been created to tell us that for all we know, there is something we do not know, something that we will never be able to know".

Recently, in India, few notable Indian architects have been opposing the entry of foreign architects as it threatens their work share, which they think should ideally belong to them. This is both disturbing and conservative in my view. Ideally, there should be a fair competition to strive for what is best for India. We can't claim ownership of territories in a globalized world. This also limits excellence. Let the stakeholders have a sound process in place of deciding and ultimately figuring out what is best for them. How can we force it top-down? I see it as a great opportunity for India in built environment to improve and excel their local practices in terms of quality, process

---

Source: World Architecture News, online. October 2012

and outcome. We are currently sitting on a huge deficit of skilled workers in built environment, and we cannot afford to reject talent pool that is coming to India from other parts of the world. Instead, there should be well-drafted policies, which are inclusive in job generation for Indians as well as foreign workers and drive towards quality.

With what the world is today, where a major chunk of opportunities lie within developing nations, it will be quite natural for businesses to be drawn to where opportunities are. Either the gates are closed or shut. Partially open gates are still open gates. The message that Indian architectural community is sending out to the world, is that we do see the need of your expertise but we feel threatened by your competence and hence our reluctant approach in welcoming you. We are being tyrannical in our approach here.

Tadao Ando was in Mumbai looking for an opportunity in architecture and he will probably be working with Godrej Properties Group on a residential project. But that is all there is to it, so far.

But given the current architectural scenario, there is so much scope for architecture and design work that we don't have to hoard and mark territories. There is room for local architects, foreign architects and hybrid architects much the same. Whatever those terms have come to mean, I say this because I do not understand their correctness in the context of our eroded identity where we have come unstuck from our roots, for better or worse, we don't know yet.

What we lack is a vision of an overall city, a holistic urban plan, and our architectural aspirations. Once we have that cleared, the smaller pieces will be easier to put together in this jumbled puzzle.

The 2013 edition of 361 Degrees Conference in Mumbai

Architectural conferences are usually made of great moments and breeding ground for exchanging ideas. The 2013 edition of the 361 Degrees Conference, which is now in its 6th year, concluded on 8th March, was no different. Over the last 5 years, 361 Degrees has aimed to capture the true essence of architecture and creating a forum where young and the old mix in a meaningful interrogation. I was particularly elated to see such a huge number of students attending the conference. The conference was well organized, kudos to the team at IA&B who took upon this colossal task.

I came back saturated with great examples and inspiration from the world of architecture. The speakers were an eclectic mix of nationalities with even more eclectic work and their individual journeys they are embarked on in built environment. On one hand, there were stalwarts like Charles Correa, who choked the audience into tears with exemplary work of Champalimaud Centre of the Unknown, Portugal and, on the other hand, were the works of the likes of Kevin Low Mark and Manuel Clavel Rojo. The message delivered was singular and a strong one: that architecture is a multi-layered discipline of social enquiry and that it can be meaningful, socially relevant and profound.

Peter Rich proposed the idea that the world is engulfed in a revolution where much of the erosion has taken place in recent history and is looking at culturally significant countries like India and Mexico to rediscover newer and deeper ways to solve many problems that we are facing as humanity.

Jenni Rueter works in the domain of enabling poor communities with the help of architecture. She has initiated several projects in Senegal where she engaged with the community first hand and works with the entire cycle of raising fund and actively involving local communities in building the project.

Kevin Mark Low said something extremely profound and notable: "Why can't buildings be as imperfect as us human beings, why are

Source: World Architecture News, online. March 2013

we so anxious to find perfection in the built environment?" I will be trying to explore and understand this more with an interview with him in a series to follow.

Graham Morrison of UK-based practice, Allies and Morrison, talked about several of his projects on buildings as not being treated as solo achievements but looking at them more as public spaces they generate – which can be both functional and engaging. He later mentioned something which is of relevance here that roads should not be treated only as means to get to places but as places themselves. This paradigm shift may relieve us from the perils that have emerged from a complex web of clinical and detached concrete urban freeways.

Lastly, I would wrap this post with a discovery of work of a Sri-Lankan Architect Palinda Kannangara. He is a man of few words and is soft spoken. His work speaks the language of almost monk-ish outcome through his projects, primarily for the residential segment. It is serene, calm and with a strong sense of geometry. His methodology appeared intuitive and visceral rather than based on any articulated design principles. His projects had a Zen-like impact and you just wanted to be there in those houses, even if it was for a brief time. Perhaps someday when Sri-Lanka beckons, I will be able to experience it.

Chapter 7

In-depth interview with architects

Kevin Mark Low

Kevin Mark Low, an architect based in Malaysia, whose work has gained global recognition, left his corporate architecture job to reclaim and pursue old dreams and establish his practice, *smallprojects* in 2002, which he runs single-handedly. He has since lectured internationally and conducted workshops and design critiques at various universities. Recently, Kevin was in India as a speaker for 361 Degrees conference where WAN's Mumbai correspondent Pallavi Shrivastava had an opportunity to speak to him. Edited excerpts from the interview:

Q: What inspired you to be an architect? And growing up as a professional architect, whose work you looked up to?

A: Many things really – my mother who taught geography, encouraged my ability to draw, without knowing that some of the worst architects in the world draw beautifully and some of the best, awfully. My father, being more taciturn, didn't appear to bother much with what I decided, but the important thing was their both supporting the decisions I made – especially my mother and whatever she saw in me at the time, which pushed me just that bit further.

Throughout architecture school and my working years, I found, I was less fascinated by architects than the specific buildings they did – over the course of my life, these were Cimitero Brion (carlo scarpa), Zimmerman House and Clooney Playhouse (Frank Lloyd Wright), Barragan House (Luis Barragan), Lunuganga and the Alfred Street house (Geoffrey Bawa), the Louvre Museum intervention (I.M. Pei), Exeter Library (Louis Kahn), the St. Louis Gateway Arch and MIT Chapel (Eero Saarinen), Casa En Valle de Bravo (Alberto Kalach), Chapel of Hope (Sigurd Lewerentz), Chapel at Ronchamp (Le Corbusier), Maison de Verre (Pierre Chareau), Commerzbank headquarters (Norman Foster) and the Cabrer house (Lacroze/

Source: World Architecture News, online. March 2013

Miguens/Prati). I feel that these architects built each work with a profound understanding of their specific context.

Of these, the work of Frank Lloyd Wright, Luis Barragan and Geoffrey Bawa are the only three whose architecture consistently engaged the aesthetics of age in the way of time passing. Perhaps, this as yet undocumented understanding had the deepest impact on my own development.

Q: You mentioned something intriguing in your talk about natural state of ways and materials in architecture and your ongoing query on why buildings can be as imperfect as us human beings? Can you elaborate on it?

A: In the way 60-year-old people look a touch strange when they try to look like 16-year-old, buildings that attempt to defy the passage of time puzzle me. I have a greater affinity for architecture that looks its age, architecture designed with sufficient confidence such that the knocks and scrapes of its making and use add instead of detract form how it is ultimately perceived. There is something about the wrinkles and lines of an old face that is beautiful, that tells its own rich story of scars, tears, joy and pride. In the same way some of us age with dignity and grace, so architecture can too – the question is what one do to encourage the circumstances under which such gracious aging happens? As such, I select materials and engage methods of construction less for how they are able to hide inaccuracy or imperfection, growth and decay, or the ravages of use, than for how all these aspects find their natural place as part of the aesthetic character, the life of the building. Perhaps I can quote from a passage I had written in smallprojects (adaptus 2010) –

"The way in which I interact with my architecture is total; friends are made of contracts and contractors, of detritus, building culture, materials and their manufacture, the act of use, of maintenance and the tectonics of construction. As friends, they are less there for the act of building than for what they intrinsically are, evidenced in the final product; one chooses not hide the nature of one's friends but to discover them over time. Design thus becomes less the act of showing than of revealing – that of the details of space and its assembly, of production, of weaknesses and strengths of materials, and the character of elemental finish. A construction effort observed to be less skilled through act or appearance is not always rectified, but is instead given integrity through the design of its relationship to its immediate physical context – the materials and processes of construction, each understood for their basic characteristics and specific applications, find expression in the tectonics of what is created. And the simple issue of time passing becomes natural; that familiarity and sense of scale that only comes with age guide my deliberations and decisions, as time has considerably less impact on the quality of light and space (as volume) than it does on the materials that reveal them. Architecture as a process does not end when the building is done, it barely begins. People age, as do materials and buildings: I am predisposed not merely to make their transition as gracious and dignified as possible, but to re-engage them in ways I never realised were possible".

Global culture has become somewhat of a beast obsessed with the novelty of form. It has certainly grown past its previous romance with the spectacle of it, but the problem still remains that if the *form* of a work fails to excite or stimulate and present *formal* experiences in some fresh way, it warrants less attention. And a great part of this zeitgeist is driven by the immediacy, the instantaneous nature of the Internet – nothing is new or fresh if it is posted a day later. As such, we have evolved an architecture of the photoshoot, of work that has to be imaged as soon and as quickly as it is completed, an architecture intended to be experienced in completeness from the first day it is inhabited. For the work I do, it is not possible for me to think of architecture as ever complete with the completion of the contract – with something as dynamic, unpredictable, and human as architecture, as architects I believe we can only ever begin what time alone can complete.

Q: Can you tell us a little bit about your project Sibu Pavilion, the thought process, context and your suggested solution? Can you share couple of pictures with World Architecture News?

A: For the Malaysian Garden Festival, held at the Lake Gardens in Kuala Lumpur in 2006, the Sibu Municipality of Sarawak in East Malaysia requested a local landscape architect for a design that was to be their pavilion. For all their lack of exposure as a somewhat marginalised logging town, the enlightened clients made request for a public toilet facility as a garden pavilion. Through his many years of work acquaintance with smallprojects and affinity for its completed work, the landscape architect took the opportunity to re-commission a working concept and design for the project.

The problem first lay in the fact that most, if not all, public toilets simply look like public toilets all over the world – commonly expressed as three blank walls with high level windows for privacy and the last remaining wall with a door for access. Unless one was to get perverse, or hide the facility behind in some manner, it was simply impossible to escape the aesthetic ubiquity of a public toilet. And so they got the original global toilet, a bush.

Sibu Pavilion

The site for the Sibu Pavilion was in the precinct of the Lake Gardens, a green enclave and city park presided over by a single large water body – the namesake for the park. Located at the foot of an old-growth Tembusu tree, the site was endowed with panoramic views across the lake to heavily verdant surrounds; a gentle slope of well-tended lawn from the access pathway to the revetment wall of the lake's edge. The north end of the pavilion became a lounge for a sofa and armchairs under the shade of a grand old Tembusu tree, with views of the lake, while the other end became a tearoom. Nestled between the two was the 'bush,' a grove of a hundred and twenty apple green Eugenia aromaticum trees sourced from a nursery in southern Malaysia. A narrow maze ran through the tightly packed trees to a squatting pan commode at the heart of the grove, guarded by the trunk of a gnarly, Indian coral tree selected from the same nursery. A compost wall of steel mesh and dead leaves, with basin niches cut into the mesh to facilitate the washing of hands, gave privacy to the entrance. Fashioned after the Archie Bunker chair from a lawn furniture competition years back, the wall was to function as a recycled leaf repository for the local council as they swept the grounds of the Lake Gardens; the dead leaves would be disposed of efficiently, with the added value of replenishing the privacy required of the toilet entrance. The temporary pavilion may have been novel, but its significance went beyond its conceptual overtones of a pun – in built form, it served as a practical template for the screening and dignity of a functional garden and park toilet facility.

 Sibu Pavilion

Evenly textured and neatly packed to the limit of its confines, the idea of the compost wall was not merely one of privacy for the bush bathroom it concealed and simultaneously announced; it was intended as a dump for park leaves and detritus, reducing the need for botanic waste transfer to a dumping ground elsewhere. The leaves and green garbage, piled on and compacted over time, begin their humid journey to decay and decomposition, to be removed at the end of the natural cycle for use as garden food; a functional and symbolic processing of park ecology. In its working form, the compost wall would have been designed with hinged lower mesh doors, from which the composted layers would be taken as a convenient source of fertilizer within the precinct of the park.

Q: Do you feel there is a larger theme unfolding beyond this east and west divisive discourse that is taking place to understand our field of architecture? What do you think of this distinction as we try to enforce traditional, modern, post-modern labels of architecture?

A: The idea of an East/West divide is a little banal really, being predicated on where someone arbitrarily decided to draw a middle line – if that longitude had been hard-lined just off the Californian coast for example, East would have been Europe, the former Soviet Union and China would have been the West, and the United States of America would be located somewhere right by the Middle East.

In preparation for a talk at the recent International Conference on Tropical Architecture in Singapore, I realised upon shading the tropical belt between the Tropic of Cancer and that of Capricorn, that the world actually found division by latitude rather than longitude – that besides the southern tips of South America and Africa, New Zealand and the nether parts of Australia, nothing was really left over of the southern hemisphere with the tropical belt shaded in – it's really either Northern Hemisphere or the Tropics. The discovery made me think about the differences of each; the northern hemisphere with its predictable and gradual temperature shifts from moderate to extreme, and the tropics with its consistently even temperature, but with more drastically changing weather patterns. And I began to figure a slightly different way to understand the global divide.

The people of the north had their lines drawn from the very beginning regarding survival – one either prepared for the long winter during the summer and fall, or died trying to keep warm and fed, since both food and fuel were scarce during the deep winter. The rigors of survival simply ensured that certain exacting concepts of order would evolve and be deeply ingrained in northern cultures and societies since life depended on it. The tropics conversely, with its moderate temperature swings and being the land of milk, honey, ukuleles and shish kebabs, has never truly developed formal systems of order of its own – if it flooded, one simply climbed a tree; hunger was merely fed by fruit; and dwelling was accomplished by the most temporary of materials since these were found in such great abundance year long. Humanity in the tropics was not bound by survival to any sense of deeper formal order. Barring exceptional conditions of filtering influences, political/cultural/social upheaval or the natural dictates of land mass in specific regions (China and central Asia, as examples), the tropical belt has resulted in cultures and societies with architectural traditions that basically took longer to develop with the same rigor, exactitude, and systemised industry of fabrication and production as that found in the northern hemisphere.

I believe that a deeper understanding of architecture cannot happen through broad and arbitrarily drawn distinctions of form – it can only be sought through deeper questions we choose to ask about content – the specificity of place, time, culture, and language. The architectural distinctions we currently have, all concern labels as related to the generalisation of formal considerations which create diametrically opposing ideas, whether it is about the east or west, traditional or modern, post-modern or deconstructivist – although some may have begun with deeper philosophical basis, they have all been reduced to, and identified by formal outcomes of expression. As such, I find architectural labels a touch silly as they mystify through formal categorisation rather than clarify through deeper involvement of content. I would rather the foundations of architecture be rooted in content and the specific context thereof, and all those issues that go beyond mere texture, colour, shape, material, space, and size.

Q: What would be your advice to young and emerging architects?

A: The world is broadly made up of two kinds of practitioners, commercial architects and critical architects. It matters less what sort of architect you decide you wish to be, but that you are absolutely honest about the decision you make. Too many architects decide that the business and branding of their architecture is what they are best at, and yet speak about their work as though design is their priority – most especially when whatever talent is available to them has brought them a measure of global success and attention. It is not wrong to compromise in life, but it is wrong to be dishonest about that act of compromise.

Conversely, if critical work is what one has decided for oneself, the understanding that patience is the deepest pursuit of true passion becomes necessary. Not fame, not success, not recognition, since none of these are about passion, nor relate to it. Passion is, not knowing where you will end, since your only care is the journey, not where it will ultimately lead you. An architectural project is like an expedition to the top of the world, Everest. If your goal is to summit for that money shot and the experience of reaching the top, then that is all you will take away with you. The most accomplished and respected climbers in the world never look at a summit as their goal, but merely as a guide for where they have to take their very next step, and strangely enough, every step focused on, creates that patience which feeds the passion. And all the best climbers in the world reflect on exactly the same experience upon their reaching the top – less the jubilation of having succeeded in what they set out to do, than the absolute surprise and excitement at finding themselves at a place they never thought they would arrive at. In the same way, commercial architects look at how far they have come, build on what they have accomplished, and are amazed at what they intend to do next. Critical architects are amazed simply at what they are currently involved in doing. But whatever the case, I believe that it is ultimately less important what one chooses to do; only that one is absolutely honest about that decision.

Q: How has Indian landscape and its cultural conditions affected you in this trip? What learning and unlearning you are taking back as architect?

A: India is very much the centre of the world. I believe the raw dictates of its culture amid the sheer mass of its population provide the perfect combination of empathy to provide a way forward for the rest of humanity, but only if it realises the way forward is not the one prescribed by the developed world – that of free capital markets, advancing the brand, pushing the boundaries of one's selected market, and sustaining the global culture of acquisition. Specifically, I have learned that on Indian roads, men, women, children, cows, pushcarts, motorcycles, cars, lorries and buses are not different types of things, but part of the amazing life of a street, and there is little difference between being nudged by another human being and a cow, or a bus, because life is simply too rich for such distinctions to matter. It is this delightful ambiguity that I will take away with me.

Q: What is state of women architects in Malaysia? Is it culturally progressive or regressive for female architects to thrive?

A: I do not believe one's sex plays much of a part in one's ability to thrive professionally in Malaysia, though it very well might in another country. Through my years working in Malaysia, I am quite glad to say that I have never experienced an intelligent statement, comment, or question by a female or male architect that was not given deep regard, and with that individual earning the greater respect of others. Perhaps the deeper aggression associated with men enables certain advances and opportunities denied women, but I believe that culture here has little to blame for.

Having taught at the University Malaya in Kuala Lumpur over the past 10 years, I have found female students to actually have an edge over male students with respect to a quicker understanding of concepts, ideas and issues of *content* over those of *form*. I do believe women have it in them to be greater architects than men. However, I also believe women to be better nurturers than men, and when it comes to raising a family, a woman will make sacrifices few men would ever consider, let alone undertake. The fact is that many of us do grow up, get married, and ultimately produce children – if there exists fewer women than men in architecture performing at the very highest levels of the profession, I believe it is only because the very best women architects are doing their best work caring for their families as a sacrifice they cannot see any other way but make.

When I previously had an opportunity to interview small projects' Kevin Mark Low for WAN, we discussed a variety of topics, from inspiration to advice for young architects and the position of women in the architectural profession. I prodded him to explain to us why he felt women are more naturally inclined as nurturer and also why towards *content* more so than *form*. His extended reply to that specific question reads as follows:

What is the state of women architects in Malaysia? It is culturally progressive or regressive for female architects to thrive?

I do not believe one's sex plays much of a part in one's ability to thrive professionally in Malaysia, though it very well might in another country. Through my years working in Malaysia, I am quite glad to say that I have never experienced an intelligent statement, comment, or question by a female or male architect that was not given deep regard, and with that individual earning the greater respect of others. Perhaps the deeper aggression associated with men enables certain advances and opportunities denied women, but I believe that culture here has little to blame for that.

Having taught at the University Malaya in Kuala Lumpur over the past 10 years, I have found female students to actually have an edge over male students with respect to a quicker understanding of concepts, ideas and issues of *content* over those of *form*. I do believe women have it in them to be greater architects than men. However, I also believe women to be better nurturers than men, and when it comes to raising a family, a woman will make sacrifices few men would ever consider, let alone undertake. The fact is that many of us do grow up, get married, and ultimately produce children – if there exists fewer women than men in architecture performing at the very highest levels of the profession, I believe it is only because the very best women architects are doing their best work caring for their families as a sacrifice they cannot see any other way but make.

Please do let me try to explain further – you see, I approach things from a considerably more biological and psychological perspective, which if you don't mind, I'll try to clarify. The human animal is, by and large, a predominantly sexually-driven one (yes, we can go on talking about the rationality and sense of self-awareness that marks human beings different from animals, but so much of what drives us is our sexuality – almost every experience of human *want* in life relates to our sexuality. Not sex, mind you, as these are two completely different things). As such, the individuals we each feel we are is very much a part of our perception of our own sexuality. And medicine has found that the hormones most responsible for determining our sexuality come from the brain. I believe it is the combination of these hormones, and human perception of the physical sexual organ most acutely associated with each sex (from the very first moment we begin to grasp concepts of space and form) that has the male mind see itself as occupying space, and the female mind as being part of it – each incidentally corresponding to how the penis is an object in the space it occupies, while the vagina is that space within, which it has nurtured/created.

Of course there are many other specific biological, social and cultural mechanisms that determine how we each perceive and relate to the creative act, but by and large, the profound depth of that psychological difference between the sexes results in men arriving at the objectification of situations much quicker, reducing problems to tangible attempts at solutions faster, whereas women take greater time to understand the abstract and conceptual aspects of any problem set before them, before any attempt at resolution is made. I must emphasize there are obvious exceptions, as nurture plays an equally important part in how each mind develops, with special circumstances affecting how certain individuals might prove otherwise, but generally speaking, and certainly within the context of Malaysia, I have found my male students to arrive at formal solutions considerably faster than their female counterparts – merit of solutions however, happily notwithstanding. As an aside, I suspect the female aspects of my psyche are more dominant than my male side of things, possibly as a result of particular circumstances in my formative years, while it might not be wrong to say your male component is a touch stronger than your female side, for the same reasons. This might not impact our intrinsic sexuality, but it well makes us a touch different from the norm.

So men lean towards objectification and women, conceptualisation. An interesting addendum to this is the fact that form is intrinsically also easier to work with than concepts, due to their tangible nature. As such, not only does objectification happen quicker and easier for men, they are simultaneously helped with it through the pure nature of form itself. It should be remembered once again though, that being quick with form doesn't necessarily mean being good with concepts.

For the reasons above, I believe that the male facility with objectification is what drives them quicker to some degree of recognition than women, as a pure default of the immediacy which form is assimilated, categorised and hailed, but also for the sad state of the world with its preoccupation with the iconisation and objectification of the same – a biologically male trait. And the fact that women are generally more inclined to engage conceptual issues (which take so much more time due to their richness) rather than immediately formal ones, simply means that they take longer and have to develop the patience to produce tangible solutions; both very difficult tasks.

Which brings me back to the point I attempted to make in my earlier reply regarding women and children – you see, more women, for the reasons I have given as the nurturers they biologically and psychologically are, simply have the patience to do what men are less capable of – raising children – in sacrifice of their careers. The more involved reason I have provided here (which I had not described earlier in reply to your question, due to its length) is something I believe to be a lesser effect of the same biological and physiological tendencies built into being either male or female.

It isn't the system that *limits* the aspirations of women; it is firstly due to innate sexuality that certain roles are naturally assumed. After that, it is the system that limits *content* in preference for *form*. The unfortunate fact is simply that women are generally more driven by content, and men, at form. As such women are marginalised by *default* of the system, not limited by *intention*.

At its most profound levels of expression, form finds nurturing through issues of content, taking deep patience and time. As is most commonly evidenced however, form develops through the subtle aggression of objectification, requiring neither considerable effort of patience nor engagement of content, and can be accomplished within short turnover of time. The latter is simply what more men than women, identify with.

Jenni Reuter

Jenni Reuter, an architect from Finland and part of Hollmén Reuter Sandman Architects, has been a strong proponent of working with neglected and marginalized communities who have an architectural expression of their own, which is locally rooted, participatory and affordable to the people it serves. Jenni also teaches at Aalto University School of Arts, Design and Architecture in, Helsinki, Finland. Jenni was in Mumbai for 361 Degrees conference where WAN's Mumbai correspondent Pallavi Shrivastava had an opportunity to speak to her. Edited excerpts from the interview:

Women Center, Senegal 1

Source: World Architecture News, online. May 2013

Women Center, Senegal 2

Women Center, Senegal 3

Q: How and when did you decide to become an architect and growing up as an architectural professional whose work inspired you in forming your own philosophy and creative style in architectural expression?

A: When I was young and thinking of what to start studying I was interested in many different fields and wasn't at all sure that architecture was my thing. But when I started studying, having really inspiring teachers such as Juhani Pallasmaa I understood that the field is so broad that you can combine very many interests in the same profession.

Q: Tell us a little bit about your architecture practice, its goals and vision and inspiring project or projects along the journey and inspiration that led to formation of Ukumbi NGO.

A: We, the Finnish architects Saija Hollmén (born 1970), Jenni Reuter (born 1972) and Helena Sandman (born 1972), started our collaboration in 1995 with the Women's Centre project in Senegal. After the completion of the Women's Centre in 2001, we understood that the fundraising for these types of projects is possible only through an NGO.

Ukumbi is a Finnish non-governmental organization established in 2007. The word Ukumbi is *Swahili* and it means a forum, veranda and a meeting place for dialogue and interaction. Our mission is to offer architectural services to communities in need. Our architectural strategy employs the use of local and traditional building techniques and customs during the planning and the construction process. Ukumbi empowers communities by involving them in the design process. Our projects are ecologically sustainable, using locally manufactured, recycled or grown building materials whenever possible. Today Ukumbi is a larger platform for several teams of architects, organizing seminars and sharing information through articles and lectures.

Our office Hollmén Reuter Sandman Architects' projects span from interiors to urban planning. We work in Finland as well as with several underprivileged communities around the world. Apart from working as visiting critics and lecturers, we also teach at the Aalto University in Helsinki.

Q: You have chosen a road less travelled to pursue architecture and your goals are not commercial but are more rooted in affordable and sustainable and indigenous practice for communities where such services are not easily

available or have been neglected. How did journey happen and what made you go this path?

A: I've always liked traveling and getting to know new cultures and places. My mother worked with an education project in Namibia in southern Africa for several years. At that time I studied architecture in Helsinki and when visiting my mother I started to study the local building traditions in Namibia and write about them. The following year there was a course organized from the department of Architecture in Helsinki University of Technology that went to Senegal on a field trip. I joined the course and started to work together with Saija Hollmén and Helena Sandman on the Women's Centre project. We got so involved with the people and the place that we started to look for funding for the project. Six years later the building was ready. It was a hard, but rewarding journey.

Q: You mentioned a project in Senegal and it was truly inspiring to see you go through the entire life-cycle of project from striving for funding to designing to execution through exploration of local materials and skills. The video you showed us at 361 deg. conference was a high point, where end-users partake in celebration with a sense of belonging. Has it been difficult to conceive such projects, which serve marginalized communities and what have been your lessons building such projects?

A: To get projects really rooted in a community and a place the process usually takes a lot of time. The fundraising is often slow as well. Unfortunately we have several projects that are not executed yet because of reasons we have little control over. For example, the revolution in Egypt that is taking place in the country. Our Learning Centre in Cairo is already designed, with the Egyptian fundraising made but we have been waiting for the building permit for several years because of the unstable situation in the country for the moment.

Q: This question was raised in conference as well and I have heard several varied opinions on it. Why do you think, we do not see more women in architecture and its allied services?

Do women choose themselves to opt-out naturally or it is something systematic that women choose not to aspire for leadership positions. Do you see changes happening in terms of it becoming gender neutral in days to come?

A: I have been teaching architecture in Finland for over 10 years and have seen very talented female and male students throughout the years. For the moment approximately half of our students are women. When I was studying we didn't have any female professors, today we have several of them. I do see a change happening, but very slowly. There is still a very strong male dominance on leadership positions which I think partly is due to the "good brother" system where men, probably unconsciously, help other men to proceed in their careers. Women very often have to convince even more to get the same position.

Q: What would your advice be to young and emerging architects and what is your one big advice that you give to your students as a teacher while teaching at Aalto University School of Arts, Design and Architecture in Finland?

A: I do think the most important thing you can do as a teacher is to get your students want to know more and get inspired by this broad and interesting profession.

Q: What has been your experience traveling to India and how has the landscape, people and its built environment affected in your broader understanding of architecture?

A: This was my first trip to India. It was a long-time dream coming true. Even though the trip was very short I had the time to see many different environments. I was privileged to give a talk at the beautiful CEPT Architecture School in Ahmedabad with some interesting professors and nice students showing me around in the wonderful city. My friend, Indian architect Bijoy Jain, was kind to invite me to his extraordinary home and workshop outside Mumbai, showing some of his extremely haptic and strong buildings.

I really hope that we will be able to work with some projects in this lovely country in the near future.

Peter Rich

Peter Rich is one of the most significant architects based in South Africa. He has extensively documented the indigenous African settlements during the Apartheid in the 1970s and this is very much the influence on his work. His work came in international focus when his documentation and analytical sketches were made public, which he deeply feels is an integral part of architectural enquiry. He has been affiliated as the Professor of Architecture at University of the Witwatersrand in Johannesburg for 30 years and he was recently a keynote speaker at 361 degrees conference in held in Mumbai. WAN's Mumbai correspondent Pallavi Shrivastava had an opportunity to speak to him. Excerpts from the interview are presented below:

Peter Rich_South Africa 1

Source: World Architecture News, online. April 2013

Peter Rich_South Africa 2

Q: Do you believe architects can be or should be geographically (whole debate of east and west) specific with their distinct inquiry, process and solutions?

A: Yes, I believe geographically physical, climatic and cultural context, provide the clues to, if responded to in an intelligent way, an enriching architecture. The challenge in a globalising world is to not be creating synonymous environments, which could be anywhere.

Q: When did realize you wanted to be an architect? What other architects/ thinkers that have greatly inspired you in your journey of architectural inquiry?

A: I was born an architect – my parents saw me as the successor or re-incarnate of my mother's brother whose architectural life was cut short at 29 years old – there was something mythically heroic and wonderful about being an architect.

Q: Where do you derive inspiration in your architecture work? You mentioned in your talk about engaging with local

community and listening to them carefully and thus moving towards to solve it architecturally. Can you elaborate a little more on it?

A: I derive inspiration from observing and through drawing trying to gain deeper understanding, be it from how ordinary people live, or good examples of architecture or from my heroes. There is much to learn, from the ordinary people who we are designing for – from the delight ordinary people experience using our creations.

Q: Globalization is being seen as one of the disruption just like wars were previously looked at. Disruption can be a great time for re-invention of people and a nation as well. You mentioned world is looking at India to come up with unique architectural philosophy to respond to solve some of the challenges. Can you talk a little bit about it?

A: India is in a unique position in the world. It is benefiting from the infrastructure and institutional structures put in place by the British and a really good educational system at all levels of learning. India some 70 years after Independence NOW has the confidence to discover itself – its Indianness – and be proud of just that. It is the place of the fresh and the new. It has its Masters in Doshi, Correa, Neelkanth Chhaya and the late architect Raje. It has its emerging masters in Bijoy Jain of Studio Mumbai, Rajeev Kathpalia and Rahul Mehrotra, to name a few. In other words it has more depth of good architects who are alive than the United States.

Q: What is your advice to young architects and designers? And which young architects you are looking up to from recent times?

A: Know who you are. Respect your circumstance culturally and climatically – learn from your masters – learn from your ancient culture and from what peasant cultures attuned to their circumstance.

Young architects I am looking up to are Alberto Kallash of Mexico, M3 of Australia, Bijoy Jain, Sanjay Mohe of India, Palinda Kannangara of Sri Lanka, Li Xianodong of China, Arturo Franco of Spain, Estudio Barozzi Veiga of Italy/Spain.

Q: Hand-drawn sketches from your travels seem to be a large part of your practice. To what extent do you use digital technology (e.g. AutoCAD and BIM) in the design process and do you think that a careful balance between the two is important in the education of the next generation of architects?

A: Use the computer intelligently as a tool. Draw your way freehand into your ideas as it gives you access to the library of your autobiography, which is not in your computer.

Q: What do you think of 3D printing?

A: It is a very useful tool.

Q: Any particular project that you would like to talk about in brief and why is it dear to you? Can you share couple of images of your project(s)?

A: The Amazwi Project – the first Women's Museum in Africa – to be built in the Valley of a thousand hills, KwaZulu Natal, South Africa. The project has evolved into a centre, which is representative of both the feminine principle and its logical extension as a centre of the environment. It is at a stage where the stakeholder dialogue is giving rise to potential built form and a dialogue between the making of the women's centre and the centre of the environment.

Sanjay Puri

Sanjay Puri Architects in one of the young leading architectural practice based in Mumbai whose work has gained international recognition. The practice is led by architect Sanjay Puri whose work has received several national and international awards for his work across India. WAN's Mumbai correspondent Pallavi Shrivasatava had a chance to speak with him about his practice, origins and his recently concluded notable project Bombay Arts Society in Bandra, Mumbai. Edited excerpts of the interview:

Q: Growing up as an architect whose work you looked up to both nationally and internationally and why? What kind of architectural philosophy from other peoples' work you have tried to imbibe and specific work that has given you great inspiration?

A: The kinds of works that are inspiring are the ones that are exploratory creating a completely different architectural language in terms of the ways their spaces are perceived. The Jewish Museum in Berlin by Daniel Libeskind, the Cinema centre in Dresden by Coop Himmelblau, the Guggenheim Museum in Bilbao and the Stata Centre in MIT, Boston, both by Frank O. Gehry are some of the most inspiring works of architecture I have experienced.

In total contrast to these relatively new projects, the old towns of Budva and Kotor and the Sveti Stefan island in Montenegro, each of them built 600 years ago and still being used today were very inspiring to me because of their organic character and the delightfully surprising spaces they possess.

In India, Fatehpur Sikri and the older parts of Jaisalmer and Jodhpur in Rajasthan too are amazing to experience as a series of interesting spaces built several years ago and yet with such a sense of contextual response.

Source: World Architecture News, online. July 2013

Q:You are one of the leading home-grown young architecture practices and your work has gained global recognition. Can you share a little bit about your journey as an architect, how it began leading to its current form and where do you see it moving in next 10 years with respect to projects, growth and firm's philosophy?

A: The journey would take many pages to describe. It has been eventful all along. I joined Architect Hafeez Contractor's office in Mumbai when he had just begun his career and I was the fourth person to join his office. When I joined, I had not yet applied to an architectural college.

Before starting college in Rachana Sansad's Academy of Architecture in Mumbai, I had already worked on housing, hotel and office interior projects and had made working drawings, supervised sites and done a lot of what qualified architects do. That beginning itself was an unbelievably enriching experience. I continued to work throughout the 5 years of college with Hafeez Contractor. Simultaneously working on hypothetical design projects in college and on real projects in office was an extremely knowledge gaining 5 years. In addition, I also started doing interior projects on my own from the 2nd year onwards. From purchasing hardware and plywood to executing designs with unskilled workers, I went through the entire process learning, making mistakes and gaining experience.

Even before my 5th year results were announced, I was made an Associate Architect and that was another landmark event. While yet working, I was approached by Ashwin Sheth of Sheth Developers, a Mumbai developer, to do some small architectural work. During one of my visits to his projects, he asked my opinion on a layout of 54 acres. Instead of just giving an opinion, I sat with him for a couple of hours re-sketching the entire layout, creating a hierarchy of spaces and generating large garden areas in the layout as opposed to the original approved one. This eventually became my first large project on the basis of which I started my own office in 1992.

In the years to come I look forward to creating large urban projects that will rejuvenate cities, while being contextual, sustainable and exploratory in the way spaces are perceived.

Q:Can you tell us little bit about Bombay Arts Society project. What was its inception like, current status and its design principles that you used for the project and involvement and inputs from client as an influencer to the project?

A: Bombay Arts Society – fluid forms enmeshed together in parts emerging from each other in parts constitute this small building.

Within an extremely small plot measuring only 1,300 sq m, a mixed use building programme based on the client's needs had to be adhered to.

Art gallery spaces, an auditorium, a cafeteria and artists rooms had to be planned within 1,000 sq m and another 1,000 sq m of office spaces were to be provided for, each with separate entrances.

Fluid spaces across the three lower levels, house the art gallery spaces and their allied functions with walls flowing into roofs homogenously. The fluidity of form seen externally, with a concrete skin encapsulating spaces while undulating in both the horizontal and vertical planes, is carried through to the interior volumes making the entire experience as that of moving through a sculpture.

A separate entrance lobby at the rear corner leads one up vertically into a four-level office space that is angled to allow the offices unrestricted views of the ocean in the distance.

The office spaces are encapsulated in a concrete skin punctuated volume with floor to ceiling glass panels in the direction of the sea.

Thus within this small 1,300 sq m plot, two distinct set of spaces are created, each with its own discernible identity and yet enmeshed together to create a uniquely sculptural building.

Q: Running an architecture firm is both business and design and everything in between. How do you balance multi-faceted aspects of the practice and are you drawn to one aspect of it more than the other?

A: Running an architectural practice, especially in India, with restricted budgets, changing rules and dealing with a general lack of awareness amongst most clients is a difficult task. If I could somehow have the requisite people to run all the business aspects, I would be happy to only concentrate on the design aspects of each project.

Q: With the influx of several international design firms finding foothold in India, do you see it as a significant influencer or game-changer in both good and not so good ways? Please elaborate.

A: It would be interesting to have design-intensive international firms doing work in India.

However, most of the international firms trying to work in India are very commercial and are not designing projects that imbibe any tradition or are in response to the climate here.

Some Developers are choosing to work with international firms only to add a perceived "brand value" to their projects. If a developer chose an international firm simply for their ability to create a new vocabulary that is contextual to India, it would make sense. However this is not the case generally.

Q: What would be your advice to young and emerging architects as a professional?

A: To create meaningful, contextual, responsive architecture and not merely follow trends.

Vinayak Bharne

Urbanist Vinayak Bharne is an Adjunct Associate Professor of Urbanism at the University of Southern California and practicing Urban Designer. His three recent books, *"The Emerging Asian City: Concomitant Urbanities & Urbanisms"*, *"Rediscovering the Hindu Temple: The Sacred Architecture and Urbanism of India"*, and the forthcoming *"Zen Spaces and Neon Places: Reflections on Japanese Architecture and Urbanism"* provide a provocative dialogues on understanding cities and city-making with their context across cultures, nations and histories. WAN's Mumbai Correspondent, Pallavi Shrivastava spoke to Bharne about the ideas, agendas and inspirations behind these efforts. Excerpts from the interview are below:

Q: Given your multiply rooted identity, you have a far more nuanced understanding of the East-West dialogue on cities that we are currently seeing taking shape. Do you think there is a much larger theme that is unfolding in urbanization than merely the geographic tirade that we tend to witness?

A: The ongoing East-West dialogue on cities is part of a much larger theme that is trying to make sense of the bewildering global scene unfolding in front of us. It is a theme that has intricate ties with complex economics, communication and foreign policy, all of which is forcing nations, cities and communities across the world to reconsider their priorities. Urbanization is part of that. As Robert Kaplan points out in his book "Monsoon", it is part of the shifting geopolitical focus of the now-departed twentieth century, where the Western Hemisphere lay front and centre. This shift is focusing strong attention on what cities in Asia, South America, etc., mean – not out of casual curiosity as has happened before, but out of sheer need and hope. This is an unprecedented theme, wherein Western architects

Source: World Architecture News, online. December 2013

and urbanists looking for work abroad will have to recognize that the work they have done and continue to do at home – good, bad or ugly – has in some ways always been connected to that abroad, because cities abroad have always looked to the West for answers even though they may deny it. In turn native urbanists abroad will now have to rethink what their cities really mean, and reconsider how to engage with them. In some ways all three of my books spark off from the urgency within this discourse.

Q: Tell us a little bit about your three books and motivation behind each of them.

A: My forthcoming book *Zen Spaces & Neon Places* brings two decades of writing and reflecting on Japan, since my first trip in 1993 as an exchange student from India. With the emergence of China and India, Japan has now dropped below the intellectual radar, when, in fact, it continues to remain a very relevant reference for our times. So this book offers a critical reinterpretation of Japan's complex built environment across history – the import of Tang Dynasty prototypes, entry of European influences, insinuation of Western democracy, rise and collapse of the economic bubble, the Fukushima Daiichi nuclear disaster – and their transformative effects in shaping and re-shaping the Japanese built landscape we see today. The intention is to provoke deeper reflections on why and how what we see today has come to be, and learn from it.

The "Emerging Asian City" was born out of a frustration: there are a lot of books with the title "Asian Cities", but they are really focused on select regions of Asia – south-east, middle-east etc. – missing the larger point. So this book brought together multi-national, multi-disciplinary scholars who were doing great work on different parts of Asia, to capture – however imperfectly – the sheer breadth and complexity of the various forces shaping cities across Asia today. This book is an argument to notice how regions across Asia, despite their differences, also have numerous overlaps – thereby offering another reading of where Asian cities are heading.

"Rediscovering the Hindu Temple" makes the point that the Hindu temple today is a lot more than just a historic, classical, sacred artefact.

In this book, we explore the controversies behind the treatises that have shaped them, and also examine their traditional architectural canons. But more importantly we look into several other dimensions of temples that are typically missed – such as their rudimentary and populist forms as wayside shrines, their presence as larger habitats, or ritualscapes devoted to prescribed and choreographed activity. We simultaneously notice them as contemporary elements, having a profound influence on the Indian metropolitan landscape. So this book provokes a dialogue on the nexus and potential of religion and other populist forces as agents and catalysts for urban transformation in India and beyond.

Q: Through your books, specifically The Emerging Asian City, did you encounter some deeper understanding while curating and writing the series which you had missed earlier?

A: I think the deeper understanding that emerged from this book was where exactly different Asian cities overlap and separate – and why. The Indian sub-continent, for instance, is historically entwined with the cultures of the Persian and Gulf region through the Islamic trajectory, as it is with China and Japan through the Buddhist one. Colonialism; post-independence nation-building; the entry and assimilation of Western democracy; informal urbanisms; sudden cities; the embrace of Modernism – these are phenomena scattered throughout urban Asia in space and time, even though their specific guises may be different. We all know how several Asian nations, after independence, built brand new modern cities as emblems of sovereignty. But six decades later, how and why are Chandigarh, Islamabad, Jakarta and Tehran different? Rapid urbanization has been a cyclical phenomenon in Asia – Japan in the 70s, Hong Kong in the 80s, Kuala Lumpur in the 90s and now Shenzhen. The forces shaping different Asian cities have been different but neither are they necessarily isolated nor regionally unique. This may seem like a pretty obvious point, but very few books have really sunk their teeth into what exactly this means.

Q: How does this understanding reflect on your practice as an urban designer while working on projects in different

regions? Where does it intersect, amalgamate and differentiate in actual design solutions and implementation? Does this make it easier or challenging given the complexities of urban fabric and issues?

A: Most of my recent professional work outside the United States – mainly the United Arab Emirates, Panama, Mauritius, Kenya and China – has been for private developers or municipalities. In other words, it has been in the mainstream layers of city making – in that, I am not dealing with impoverished or alternative contexts, or conversely iconic high-budget creations. In this middle layer, the general ideas we promote in the United States – pedestrian-friendly streets, compact development, multi-modality, dignified density etc. – are relevant globally, because sprawl is a global phenomenon. The specifics of sprawl, however, both in form and the processes and expectations that generate it, are different across the world. So the challenge of working abroad in this respect has been one of negotiating where to introduce progressive urbanism ideas from the United States authoritatively, where not to, and where and how to adapt them. For instance in China, if you want to make a neighbourhood with small blocks and therefore more streets, many of these streets have to be private and contained within gated mega-blocks. And ultimately how to penetrate the administrative structures of a city and influence and transform planning regulation from being sprawl-driven to something else remains at the heart of all such efforts.

But I like to think that I am also engaged in another form of practice – and that is research with my students and academic colleagues. This is where I get to engage with issues beyond mainstream city-making. And this is where I get to test many of the ideas I write about. We have an ongoing research project to chart multi-disciplinary strategies for the future of Banaras, one of India's oldest sacred cities. I have a grant to do an incremental enhancement plan for the surroundings of the Ise Jingu, one of Japan's oldest Shinto shrines. We have been studying how to reuse and resurrect the ancient Qanats (subterranean water channels) of Yazd, Iran. I think all these are forms of practice – in that we are engaged in urban change and intervention, whether it is a developer project, or a hypothetical proposition.

Q: Do you see the flattening of cultural differences and the slow disintegration of diversity under the rubric of globalization as a challenge or a fertile phenomenon that may give emergence to something more interesting in cities of tomorrow?

A: I think it is both. The flattening of cultural differences began with modernization, but could not surpass the deep-rooted cultural blueprints of many non-Western cultures. In the book Emerging Asian Cities, there are several chapters that show how cultural blueprints endure. They end up becoming commodities for tourism and entertainment – as Kasama Polakit points out in her chapter on the Bang villages of Thailand. They can in fact be reinforced and renewed through successive external transformations, as Robert Cowherd observes in his piece on Surakarta. Jeff Hou examines the juxtaposition of what he calls "vertical urbanism, horizontal urbanity" – in Tokyo, Hong Kong, Taipei, etc. – where shimmering high-rises rub shoulders with a tradition of informal markets. Vic Liptak follows three generations of a native family in Aksaray, Turkey, as they renounce their traditional homes and move to new apartments, and seamlessly appropriate it with indigenous spatial patterns. Even cities like Chandigarh, as I argue in one of the chapters that were built from scratch as new utopias have been seamlessly appropriated by a native ethos. In other words, if we learn to see globalization as the continuing legacy of colonialism and modernism, then cultural resiliency is an integral part of that continuum.

Q: Rapid urbanization gives rise to unprecedented pressure on infrastructure and transport means. Which emerging/developing city according to you has tackled this challenge in a best and worst way? And why do you think so? And which developed city according to you had to go back and re-work their strategies to rising or changing needs?

A: I think most developing cities across the world are being ravaged even as we speak by placeless transportation infrastructure. This is why a city like Curitiba, Brazil stands out. Their 1966 master plan proposed a siphoned urban growth along five structural axes radiating from the urban core, but instead of focusing their infrastructure solely on cars, they initiated a rapid bus mass transit system in the central lanes of these corridors that has now gained global attention. What is less known, however, is that the land fronting these transit corridors was simultaneously zoned for high-rise buildings with residential/office uses above and retail/commercial uses at street level guaranteeing that the fabric would not only produce but also attract transit trips. Further, to incentivize the plan's implementation, the zoning was changed to permit little to no development in downtown Curitiba, whilst promoting high-density mixed-use development along these transit axes. This strategy has not been immune to capital pressures, and the development of these corridors is a far cry from the controlled consistency seen in the best western cities. But this synergistic transit-infrastructure-development strategy in a less-developed socio-economic context, implemented through a non-speculative and formal planning means is something many other cities should learn from.

For the second part of your question, Los Angeles (LA) comes to mind. Its ongoing rail transit renaissance is actually quite ironic. Barely five decades ago, Southern California had one of the most extensive train networks in the world. But the 1,000-odd miles of rail were gradually dismantled, and circa 1963 closed in favour of an extensive freeway system. As part of Los Angeles' renewed inclination towards walkability, mixed–use and non-utopian urbanisms, numerous policies are now not only advancing mass transit, but transit-oriented development (TOD) at all scales. Of course, compared to other US cities, this TOD rhetoric is miniscule, because the automobile still remains the convenient choice to traverse LA's vast distances. And with conventional zoning still regulating most transit nodes, the idea of introducing density and mixed-use around train stations remains a difficult territory, with progressive developers needing to negotiate new concepts of density and liveability through mainstream planning channels. But what is happening in LA is important. The efforts and struggles of this region can provide real lessons to numerous cities across the world.

Q:What do you think is one of biggest challenges facing the transportation sector in various cities of the world? Why? And are there few basic measures that cities can take to improve their transport networks?

A: In the United States, where regulation is everything, we are simply trying to reduce dependence on the automobile and repair the physical damage wrought by decades of regulated but myopically planned infrastructure designed exclusively for cars. In many other countries, one of biggest challenge is precisely reinforcement and regulation. So there are significant differences. But I think one challenge that unifies cities across the world is how to get transportation sectors to talk to other sectors of city planning (and vice versa) before implementing anything. This is something every city can actually do. If you are planning a highway, how can you simultaneously anticipate strategies for economic development, how can you rethink zoning around a new transit corridor right away – not as an after-thought as it is often done. In other words, how can transportation (and all other) sectors of a city-planning department stop working in isolation as if the others did not matter.

Q: Do you think people take on the identity of the city or a city takes on the identity of people who inhabit it? Do you think the identity of the city is static or something constantly transforming and evolving?

A: All cities are phenomena in flux. So how can the identity of a city be static? Granted, some cities change faster or more dramatically than others, but ultimately they are all events in time. The Japanese architect Toyo Ito had once remarked, "if a Western city is a museum, the Japanese city is a theatre". He was referring to the relative permanence of a European city versus a far more ephemeral city like Tokyo, where land scarcity compels constant demolition and rebuilding. Physically, Tokyo changes dramatically every few years. On the other hand, I am reminded of Venice, where in 1902, the campanile in St. Mark's Piazza collapsed for the second time. And even as a heated debate ensued about its future, the citizens and elected officials simply decided to replicate the fallen icon, so that the visual image of the city would be the same.

The socio-physical disposition of every city influences its inhabitants only as much as they influence it. The thing that interests me here is what I like to call urban immunity. Japanese citizens, for instance, have since historic times lived with the idea that their cities will be destroyed from time to time and rebuilt again – this is unthinkable for many of us. When people from highly regulated cities visit less regulated ones, they react immediately to ad hoc development, unhygienic surrounds, etc. But for the inhabitants of that city, it is part and parcel of daily life. The identity of a city does not stem only from icons and monuments, but equally from the deeper psychological structures and expectations of its people.

Q: As a researcher and academician, which is one of the most interesting cities that you see yourself going back for your ongoing queries and seeking answers? Please elaborate.

A: I would say Tokyo. As I write in the final chapter of my Japan book, for most non-Japanese architects and urbanists, particularly from the West, Tokyo epitomizes the extremities of contemporary urbanism. The cost of living is more than 50% higher than New York. The amount of private space per capita is 66% lower. Parks constitute merely 5% of its land surface in comparison to 30% in London. But despite these delirious densities, the amount of space actually occupied by its over-nine-million occupants on its 622-sq-km spread is only around 52% (though it rises up to 70% in central areas). Of course, none of these extreme numbers mean anything to most Tokyoites, for whom, the city is in fact a mosaic of discrete social worlds, urban neighbourhoods, streets, destinations, efficient trains, and thousands of social places. I find Tokyo very similar to Mumbai in its pace and visual intensity, but far closer to a European city when we look at its cleanliness, order and daily efficiency. For me Tokyo is one of most liveable and walkable cities in the world, even though it has evolved largely without formal planning and where one lives with the knowledge that its destruction can come at any moment. I continue to find this very intriguing because it challenges how we make, experience and live in cities, physically and mentally.

Q: What is your advice to young and emerging professionals in urban design and planning around the world and what suggested readings you would recommend them to not miss in understanding the subject?

A: Some days ago, an experienced planner put up a list of what he considers to be the 100 best books on city-making ever written. The list has all the obvious suspects and classics – from Jane Jacobs and Camillo Sitte to Andres Duany and Rem Koolhas – and attests to the vast and impressive scholarship on the subject of city-making over the past few decades. But for me, it suggests equally the shocking and dangerous Western-centric provincialism and intellectual dominance that pervades the idea of the "good city" globally – even at a time when transnational fluidity is less viscous than ever before. This is a gap that needs serious attention over the next decade by emerging professionals.

We also need urbanism and planning heroes beyond European and American ones. If you think about it, most figures beyond the West that have gained a global profile have been architects, not urbanists or planners, even though they may claim to be so. They have not really been invested in the complexities of city-making as much as making great buildings. If you look at their monographs, they are really about buildings as objects or isolated projects with nothing about processes or engagements in city making. I think the agenda of urbanism has not really attained clarity or dominance beyond the West, and even for a layperson, the idea of an urbanist or city-planner remains vague at best. If the 21st century is the century of cities, then this is the biggest task at hand – to make urbanism the real agenda of our times, to prioritize urbanism before architecture, and to help citizens understand that cities are not made by architects, but by many other actors and entities.

Acknowledgments

I would like to thank **Copal Publishing** for taking up the endeavour of putting together all my writings in a form of a book. I would like to thank **Kevin Mark Low** for going through essays and writings and providing valuable feedback from time to time and then penning the foreword for this collection. Through the interaction with him over time, I have come to learn a great deal. I would like to extend my deepest gratitude to **Prof. Christopher Benninger** for providing such wonderful words of encouragement on this book.

Last but not the least, I would like to sincerely thank **Rahul Kulkarni** for painstakingly going through the whole collection and editing it and also designing a beautiful cover for this book. Without Rahul's help, the book wouldn't have moved forward meaningfully.

Pallavi Shrivastava

About the Author

Pallavi Shrivastava is an architectural designer, currently based in Mumbai. Pallavi has been writing as an architecture and design critic for various platforms, and her writings have appeared on World Architecture News, Global Urbanist and several other professional mediums. She holds a masters degree from Arizona State University and has worked in the United States and India for various architecture and design firms.

Pallavi is passionate about human ecology and sustainability in built environment. With her writings, she likes to probe issues of culture, heritage and identity in architecture, design and urban planning under the rubric of built environment.

www.ingramcontent.com/pod-product-compliance
Lightning Source LLC
Chambersburg PA
CBHW030852270326
41928CB00008B/1333